FROM HIS PARTNER TO HIS PREY

FROM HIS PARTNER TO HIS PREY

SHAY COLE

Creative Chameleon

To request permissions, contact the publisher at acreativechameleon@gmail.com.

Paperback: 978-1-7378961-0-4
Audiobook: 978-1-7378961-2-8
Ebook: 978-1-7378961-1-1

First paperback edition October 2021.

Edited by Christie Hall, Kara Watson, Naya Perry-Eddings
Cover art by Tametra Little
Foreword by Naya Perry-Eddings
Layout by Shaquanda Cole

Creative Chameleon, LLC
Goodlettsville, TN 37072

www.acreativechameleon.com

CONTENTS

PREFACE

Many years ago I learned that I did not live my life for myself alone. I knew that I had a duty to speak for those who could not speak for themselves. I knew that I had to break the silence and have the difficult conversations. I knew that telling my story would help someone else survive theirs. Many people looked at me and saw a strong woman who could handle anything. What many people didn't know is how hard it was to keep smiling when I was breaking down inside. My journey revealed to me that everyone is not worthy of my time, love, energy, or presence. It was a hard pill to swallow because people started to disappear. Some of the same people who I though would never leave me where gone with the wind. Nevertheless, I knew I wanted to share my story. When I first started writing the book it was roughly 3 years after the divorce and I was still very close to the pain. It took time for me to heal and really learn to love myself again before I could compete this book. My goal is to start the discussion and keep the lines of communication open. I do not want others to suffer in silence hoping someone recognizes the signs of abuse and sends help.

FOREWORD

When I was asked by Shay to do her foreword I was nervous! Yet excited. I met Shay in elementary school. We didn't hit it off right then, but I could tell she was destined for greatness. She was loud! We went to all the same schools but in high school we became BEST of friends!! Graduated, lost touch, reconnected and now we are here!

While reading this book I had so many emotions going through my soul. I became engulfed with the story and put myself in the main character's shoes. As if it was me. Yes some parts angered me! There were so many loops and obstacles, within that there was no way to figure out what was going to happen next without turning the page.

I have so many connections to the book that, it angers me how things were being handled. But when you look at the big picture it gave the push that was needed to come out on top. I too was in the military; the same branch as Tyler (the husband). So I know a little bit about rules and regulations, or so I thought. In the book, this is where power presents it's ugly little lies. All while the main character Keisha exhibits diligence! She refused to let her kids see her struggle even though the struggle was real. She kept smiling through the pains and misunderstandings of her life. Not all was bad, but when it was, IT WAS! As a domestic violence survivor myself, this book gives hope and a little guidance to those who have to tackle their situation ALONE.

Strap in because this book is about strength, growth, power, and the will to not give up but more so keep going and don't settle for less! You are entering a rollercoaster of life's up and downs, military coverups, lies, betrayal, family, the struggle to keep it together and find your VOICE!

Naya Perry-Eddings

ACKNOWLEDGEMENTS

First I thank Yah for bringing me to a place of peace and allowing me to share my story with the world. I am grateful to have the support of my children, family, and friends. I greatly appreciate my friend, my homie, my business partner Tametra Little for seeing my vision and creating a dynamic cover for this project. I would like to send a major thank you to Naya Eddings for supporting me and proving the foreword for the book, I truly appreciate you. Thank you to Christie Hall and Kara Watson for helping me with editing and finalizing the book. I cannot forget to thank Mr. Jordan for his love and support as I finished up, your encouragement carried me a long way. I want to thank my entire team who has been rocking with me and keeping me focused on doing what I was sent to do. I would like to thank those who listened to my tears and pushed me to move forward. This book addresses some serious issues with abuse, domestic violence, and overall survival. I am grateful that I have survived and I can be of assistance to others who are on their journey as well.

CHAPTER ONE

Keisha & Tyler

Keisha was born in the early 80's to Gerald and Patricia Eady. Before they were married, Gerald had fathered six kids and Patricia had three of her own before Keisha came along. Soon after her birth, things changed from bad to worst. Within the first year of her life, Keisha's parents divorced, and she was split between two residences on the west side of Detroit. By the time Keisha was 14 years old, she had already lived a very traumatic life. She was molested by her older cousin when she was six. From age nine until eleven, she was sexually abused by her piano teacher, who was a close friend of the family. When Keisha turned 12, she started drinking to numb the pain. No matter how hard she tried, nothing took away the pain that was deeply rooted inside of her. Just when she felt like things were at their worst, she woke up to news that her best friend had been murdered just days after her 13th birthday. Keisha was no stranger to pain, disappointment, or death. By the time she reached high school, she had made up in her mind to get away from her neighborhood, her family, and her pain. She was smart and maintained a 3.5 grade point average or higher from elementary through high school. Her good grades often afforded her opportunities to participate in advanced programs and extracurricular activities. She enjoyed being involved in sports but was very shy in social settings.

Tyler was born in the same month as Keisha, but he was two years older. He was the second eldest son born to his parents. He was very close to his mother but had an estranged relationship with his father. Tyler was always the one who did things first among his siblings. He was the first child to see his father abuse his mother. He was also the first and only child who ever defended her. No matter what, he was on her side and always came to her rescue. His father was not around a lot because he was splitting his time between two families. Tyler liked that his father was gone a lot because that meant he didn't have to deal with him abusing his mother. Tyler was 14 when he started standing up to his father. After that, he never really maintained positive relationships with men. When Tyler turned 16, he was faced with the most difficult decision of his life. On the night of his birthday party, his parents got into a huge argument. Tyler's dad was upset because his wife did not get the cake he liked. His dad was so upset that he smashed the remainder of the cake in his wife's face, knocking her onto the floor. Tyler heard the commotion in the kitchen and walked in. Just as he opened the door, he saw his father back slap his mother and spit on her. Tyler was so angry he charged towards his father and pinned his father against the sink.

"Oh, you think you big and bad enough to step to me?!" his dad shouted.

Before Tyler could respond, he was wiping blood from his lip. His father punched him straight in the mouth.

"Mind ya' business boy, this ain't what you want!". Tyler attempted to swing on his father, but his mother stopped him.

"Don't do it Ty! I'm ok baby. See? I'm alright", his mother said as she continued to wipe cake, blood, and spit from her face.

"I can't stay here and watch him kill you Momma! I can't! Imma kill him!", Tyler screamed to his mother.

In that moment, he had to decide whether to stay and do nothing or leave and completely disengage from his family. Tyler left that night. Although they lived miles apart, Keisha and Tyler were experiencing similar amounts of immense pain, destruction, and turmoil. They both had to learn a lot about life on their own with little to no guidance. They both longed for affection, attention, and acceptance. Keisha looked for those things from everyone she met. Although she was brutally honest times, she was extremely vulnerable. She couldn't always decipher the real from the fake. She took people at their word. Tyler, on the other hand, was very guarded after he moved out. He was homeless in his hometown for nearly six months before being accepted into an employment training program a few cities away. He stayed to himself and didn't engage with many of the other students in the program.

Both Tyler and Keisha felt that they were going through the hardest part of their lives. Keisha was in love with her high school boyfriend from her junior year of high school through her second year of college before she ended their relationship.

Before their breakup, she thought she would be with him for-ever, especially after he popped up at her job and proposed to her. She learned quickly that his proposal was merely a ploy to keep her from leaving him. Once she realized that, she ended it. Keisha moved on and dated someone else.

One day, her ex-fiancé showed up at her campus apartment. He started banging on her window and demanded to be let into the apartment without regard for anyone or anything. Keisha's new friend was immediately startled and went to the opposite side of the apartment to avoid an altercation with Keisha's ex. Her ex walked into the building behind another resident and repeatedly banged on the door. Keisha listened from her room with her door locked, all alone and afraid. Unbeknownst to Keisha, while she was in her room, her roommate opened the door. Keisha's ex attempted to grill her roommates to find out where Keisha was and why no one would let him in. One of Keisha's roommates was able to finally calm him down and get him to leave before Keisha came out of her room. It was a terrifying experience that she wanted to forget as soon as it happened.

Meanwhile, Tyler was discovering various ways to provide for himself. He sold weed to his classmates, cut hair, cooked food, and wrote papers for money. He was determined to live a life better than the one he came from. While he was well off financially, he lacked the love he craved. Tyler was afraid to love because he felt like love would always betray him. For that reason, Tyler didn't trust many people. By the time they reached the ages of 18 and 20, respectively, Keisha and Tyler had lived a life full of tough decisions. They lived life separately, clueless of the other's issues. Soon enough though, their paths would cross.

The time finally arrived for Keisha to start her last year of college. She was so excited that she was closer to her goals that she decided to attend more campus events as a personal reward. In the past, Keisha avoided most campus events because she was trying to stay focused and study. When she was close to the end of her junior year, she was almost kicked out of college and nearly lost everything. She lived on campus and her student loans did not cover her housing during the summer. She owed over $5,000 and had no clue of how she was going to pay it. Her parents had told her not to stay for the summer. Keisha tried everything she could think of to get the money, but nothing came through... until she talked to her advisor. After she explained her situation, she was allowed to register for class after working out a payment plan to cover the balance while she finished school. To help pay off the balance, Keisha got a job working in the Student Union Welcome Center as a greeter. The welcome center was near the food court, and it was where most of the campus activities took place. Keisha was excited to be in the center of all the action after a rough start to her senior year.

Tyler completed the requirements for his job training program and was able to attend a nearby college. Although Tyler focused on women more than class, he graduated with a degree in communications. He attended college with a few of the guys he met while in the job training program. One of the guys, Josh, was also heavily involved in street hustling. Josh and Tyler were almost kicked out of the job training program when another student reported them to the authorities. Tyler told Josh that the guy was always looking suspect and warned Josh to stay away from him. Josh was not interested in taking Tyler's advice and served the guy anyway. Two days later, Josh and Tyler's room was searched. The only thing that saved Josh and Tyler from being discovered and expelled was Tyler's suspicious thoughts. He didn't trust the guy and he knew Josh like the back of his hand. Tyler removed everything incriminating from the room when Josh left to serve old boy...he knew dude was up to something. After their room was raided, Tyler decided to issue a few stitches to the snitch. All this happened at the end of their time in the program. Josh and Tyler graduated a week later and agreed to leave this situation behind.

Tyler and Keisha both faced a great deal of opposition to get to where they were. Although they were oblivious to one another, their paths were closer than they realized. One day, during homecoming week, Keisha and her sorority sisters set up an information table in the student union alongside the other campus organizations and clubs. This event occurred every year to attract other students to join current members. Keisha had never able to work the table before because of her class and work schedule. This year was the first year Keisha was able to work the information table with her sorority sisters instead of working at the welcome center alone. Towards the end of the day, Keisha noticed a guy walking past her sorority table. She noticed him walking past a few times but didn't think anything of it. Keisha's sorority sister, Tiffany, pointed out that he was walking past yet again. The next time he walked past, he walked closer to the table and stopped. Most of the girls thought he was interested in Tiffany since they were making eye contact the entire time he was walking past, scoping everyone out.

"Excuse me, may I speak to you privately for a moment?" Tyler asked Tiffany.

Her scowl turned into a smile, and she agreed to speak with him. They were gone for about fifteen minutes. Everyone thought they were really getting to know one another since they had been gone so long. One of Keisha's sorors asked her what time it was, and Keisha looked in her purse to retrieve her phone to report the time. When she lifted her head, Tiffany was walking up to the table with a big stupid smile and an even bigger bouquet of flowers.

"OK Soror, I see you!" Jamiya shouted to Tiffany.

Other sorors started joining in and shouting. One of them snapped her fingers to the side repeatedly and screamed out "YAAAAASSSSSSSSSSSS!"

"Alright   Soror...don't   hurt   'em!" another shouted with approval.

"Well damn Tiff! You doing 'em like that?!?" exclaimed another line sister.

Tiffany just kept smiling without saying a word until she finally reached the table. She sat the bouquet down and took the card off. She held it in her hand briefly and then she gave the card to Keisha. Keisha looked surprised as she took the card from Tiffany. When she read it, she saw her name on the outside of the envelope.

"Open it!" Tiffany urged Keisha.

Keisha was so confused. She thought that Tiffany went off with old boy to get to know him for herself and instead, Tiffany returned with a big smile and flowers for Keisha.

"Girl, what is this?" Keisha asked Tiffany

"Open it and see." Tiffany responded.

Keisha had no clue what all this was about, but she listened to Tiffany and opened the envelope. What was written on the card was even more beautiful than the flowers that came with it. It read:

Keisha,

These flowers are a symbol of how I see you. Trust and believe, the words that follow are true. Your natural beauty is what attracted me. A beauty that the heart feels and the eyes can see. A beauty that speaks on its own. A beauty that will never die. Share your beauty in my world and give my heart a try.

-Tyler

After Keisha read the card, she looked up at her sorors, who were staring intently at her. They all wore the same look on their faces.

"He's sitting over there." Tiffany finally broke the silence.

Keisha didn't say a word...she just followed the direction of Tiffany's finger as she pointed out his table. The closer Keisha got to the table, the heavier her feet felt. Her heart rate increased, and her mind was going wild. When she reached the table, he stood up.

"Thank you for coming to sit with me Keisha. Would you like something to drink?" he asked as he pushed her chair into the table.

"I'll take some water please. Thank you. Oh, thank you for

the card and flowers also. I really appreciate them." Keisha responded.

"My pleasure, Beautiful" Tyler turned and responded to Keisha before getting her water.

They sat and talked for so long that they were the last ones left in the student center. Once they realized everyone was gone, Tyler asked to walk Keisha to her apartment, and she said yes. They walked slowly and talked more about their goals and dreams and so many other things. It was something that Keisha had never experienced before. She was enjoying every moment! They sat outside of Keisha's apartment and talked some more. It was amazing...they had so much in common. They had a lot of the same hobbies and similar goals. Before they knew it, it was 2am! Keisha gave Tyler her number and ended their night together with a hug and kiss on Tyler's cheek. Before Keisha went inside, Tyler asked her what her plans were for the next day. She told him about the scheduled community service event at a local nursing home with her sorors. Tyler revealed that his uncle lived at that nursing home.

"So maybe I'll see you in a few hours." Keisha said and smiled.

"Maybe," Tyler responded with a grin.

He grabbed her hand and held it for a moment before he left. Keisha gazed at what seemed to be a perfect man (if there ever was one). Before Keisha could go into her apartment, Tyler turned around and called her name. She stopped in her tracks.

"Yes", she said softly as Tyler walked towards her.

The moon was caressing his skin and his eyes were fixed

on hers. He smelled like the perfect blend of mahogany and teakwood. His hands reached out and grabbed hers to pull her closer. At that moment, Tyler's lips spoke softly and asked for another hug before leaving. Keisha's mind was racing, and her body was tingling. She wanted to hug him all night long. Keisha leaned in and slowly moved her hands up his arms and interlocked her fingers around his neck. His hands slid down her sides and around her back. He rubbed the top of her booty as he rested his hands and embraced her.

"Thank you", he whispered.

"For what?" Keisha said.

"For allowing me the opportunity to be in your presence." Tyler said.

"You're welcome and thank you for a wonderful experience, Tyler. I enjoyed your company." Keisha responded.

"The pleasure was all mine Beautiful. I'll holla at you later Keisha. Have a great day tomorrow." Tyler said as he walked away.

"You too Tyler." Keisha said before she closed the door.

This was the beginning.

Keisha and Tyler were inseparable from the day they met. Keisha felt like she had finally met a man worthy of her. She felt like she had someone who would cherish her and treat her the way she deserved to be treated. She was so happy to have Tyler in her life and Tyler felt the same way about Keisha. He was not surprised that things were going so well. He just knew that they would. Tyler and Keisha dated for a few months before Keisha told Tyler she wanted him to meet her family. Although Tyler was very happy being with Keisha, he was not excited about meeting her family. Tyler did not have a good relationship with his own family so for that and other reasons, Tyler put off meeting Keisha's family for as long as he could. Keisha didn't understand what the big deal was about Tyler meeting her family. After a few times of asking, Keisha started to feel some kind a way because Tyler kept avoiding her family. Keisha attempted to talk to Tyler about it and he refused. He was very adamant about it just being the two of them.

"We all we got Keisha!" Tyler would tell her.

Once Keisha stopped asking Tyler to meet her family, she started asking him about the future of their relationship. Tyler did not like this kind of questioning at all. He was aggravated more by Keisha wanting more from the relationship overall. Tyler knew he liked Keisha and wanted to be with her, but what he didn't like was all the pressure he felt around the relationship. Keisha could tell that Tyler was starting to pull back and it bothered her. Although she was a little hurt by the way Tyler was acting and reacting, she didn't change. Keisha was always internalizing things that happened to her instead of reacting to them. It was easier for her to handle life that way. She hoped that things would change so she felt like she didn't have to make any adjustments.

Keisha started to trust Tyler less and less as the months passed and they were still in the same place. She felt like it was time to start pulling back because Tyler didn't want to meet her family, talk about their relationship, or their future. He wanted to do things "Tyler's way". If he didn't want to do something, he didn't do it. He felt as if it was his way or no way at all. That was how it had worked with all the other women he had dated. Keisha saw a difference in Tyler from when she was introduced to him in the student center. What she didn't know was that this is just how Tyler treated women. He knew how to get them to fall head over hills in love with him. He used his looks and his charm to his advantage. He knew just what to do to get the results he wanted. Keisha had no idea what she had gotten herself into.

One day, Tyler told Keisha to meet him at a local restaurant after her shift at the student center. When Keisha arrived, there was a group of people sitting at a table with Tyler.

"Over here babe!" Tyler shouted as he stood up and waved Keisha over to their table.

Keisha walked over slowly feeling confused about what was going on. She reached the table and greeted everyone as she made her way to Tyler. When she reached him, he introduced her to the group.

"Everyone...This is my future wife, Keisha." The look on Keisha's face was priceless. She was completely blind sighted by his introduction.

"Future wife, huh?" She whispered to Tyler after she greeted the crowd.

Tyler smiled and kept the conversation going with the group. They ate, they laughed, they talked, and then everyone met in the parking lot to say their goodbyes. Keisha's mind was blown! This was the first time Tyler introduced her to people the way that he did. She felt like he was finally coming around and she didn't have to question the direction of their relationship anymore. That introduction was the validation Keisha didn't know that she was looking for. She felt like Tyler was finally understanding why she wanted him to meet her family and was clear about their future. Tyler knew that he wanted to be with Keisha, but he didn't want her to pressure him into making decisions or meeting anyone before he was ready. He also knew that introducing Keisha as his future wife would buy him some time with her and relieve the stress they were both feeling...but at the same time, Tyler knew Keisha would not be around for much longer if he didn't do something. A few weeks later, Josh and Tyler went to campus for an event. Josh heard about the way Tyler introduced Keisha to the rest of their friends.

"Yo man, let me ask you something." Josh said to Tyler.

"Wassup?" Tyler responded.

"Why did you introduce Keisha as your 'future wife' when she met the crew?" Josh asked.

Tyler knew this question was coming but he was not interested in explaining himself to Josh.

"Cause she my girl man. How should I have introduced her?" Tyler asked with a slight attitude.

"Man, you should have just said she was your girl! Why put all that extra sauce on it?" Josh answered with conviction and concern.

"Do you really want to get married to Keisha?"

"I think so man." I'm still tryna' figure that out." Tyler answered with hesitation.

Josh pulled into the campus apartments and parked. He slowly turned to Tyler and said, "Aye man, what you do with that herb? I need to smoke for this conversation."

Tyler rolled up and gave it to Josh to spark.

"Man, what are you doing? Are you really about to marry this girl?" Josh asked.

"Yo! I like her man. She is a cool chick. I mean..."

"Man, you ain't said "yes" not one time!" Josh interrupted.

"Man! I know what I'm doing!" Tyler said as he reached for the blunt.

He smoked for about 3 minutes in silence.

He knew what he was doing but he didn't want to keep answering Josh's questions.

"Well, pass the blunt then and quit thinking so hard about." Josh was silenced because just at that moment Keisha and 2 of her sorors walked past. He couldn't finish his sentence when he saw Keisha. He hit the blunt and passed it back to Tyler.

"I know what I gotta do dawg!" Tyler told him as he blew out some smoke.

Tyler looked at Keisha as she walked to the mailbox and smiled.

"I gotta keep her man. She is a cool ass chick and I really like her. I could see us being together. She got me hooked Dawg", Tyler revealed.

"Damn man." Josh replied.

"I gotta keep her around man. I can't lose her Dawg." Tyler told Josh.

Tyler and Josh talked for about an hour in the parking lot. Tyler explained to Josh how he felt about Keisha, and he wanted to have her forever. Josh listened and gave his opinion about the situation overall. Regardless of what Josh said, Tyler was only concerned with keeping Keisha around. Josh couldn't understand why Tyler wanted Keisha so bad and why he was willing to go to such great lengths to keep her around. Since it was Tyler's choice, Josh shut up and listened as Tyler told him why getting Keisha pregnant was the best way to keep her. It was a wild idea, but Tyler felt like it was smart. It meant that no matter what, he would be tied to Keisha for life. He wanted to be in her life forever. He wanted to make sure that there was a bond that they couldn't separate from.

Tyler told Josh about his plan to get Keisha pregnant in the next few months while things were still good with them. Keisha's constant talk about meeting her family inspired Tyler to want a family of his own and he was excited about the idea. Keisha made Tyler feel loved and accepted when others looked at him like the "black sheep". He loved what she did for him and how she made him feel. She was very giving and loving. She would always go above and beyond to make sure the people she loved felt love unconditionally. Tyler never felt love the way he experienced love from Keisha. He could sense her commitment to him. She was very loyal and understanding. She balanced him and he liked having that balance.

Josh and Tyler drove around and smoked for a few more hours before calling it a night. Josh couldn't believe all that Tyler was saying to him, but he had Tyler's back, no matter what. Eventually, he wished him well with his plans and said he hoped that everything would work out well. Tyler knew what that meant, but he accepted it anyway. A few days later, Tyler took Keisha out on a date. They went to dinner and had a great time together. He was thinking about his conversation with Josh and attempting to enjoy the evening with Keisha. He knew that if he told her what was distracting him, it would scare her off.

He feared that she would be extra cautious about them

using protection or not giving it up to him at all. After dinner, Keisha invited Tyler into her apartment for a night cap. Her roommates were all away for the weekend. She lit some candles and went to take a shower. She came back into the room, wrapped in her towel, with her skin saturated with shea butter. The glow from the candle gave Keisha's skin a beautiful bronze shimmer. Tyler laid her down and made love to her. He stroked her slow and whispered "I want you to have my baby." Keisha heard what Tyler said but she didn't think anything of it because people always said wild stuff during sex...especially good sex! Keisha just kept moaning and enjoying every stroke.

It didn't take long for things to go from feeling good to being really bad. A few months after their passionate night, Keisha was forced to leave school. Although she was working off her debt, her balance grew higher than what she could pay on her own and she was unable to register for classes. She was devastated but thankful that her cousin lived by the school. Keisha asked if she could live with her cousin while she paid down her bill so that she could stay close to Tyler. Tyler was sleeping on Josh's couch at the time and was not able to do much to help Keisha. They did their best to keep in touch with one another and made sure they were able to see each other when time permitted. One day while Keisha was at her cousin's house, her other cousin Sasha came to her afraid that she was pregnant. Again!

Sasha was still dealing with her emotional wounds of having recently aborted a child, not to mention that she was at an age where she could not fully care for herself. She told Keisha she wanted to find out for sure, so they went to the store and got 2 pregnancy tests. They were so focused on getting the tests to the house, they left them on the kitchen counter. When Sasha's parents came home, they instantly went to Keisha to find out who needed the pregnancy tests. Keisha quickly claimed them to protect Sasha. Keisha was given 48 hours to reveal the results of the tests. Keisha stayed calm because she didn't have anything to worry about as far as the tests were concerned but at the same time, she was worried about Sasha. The next day, as soon as she got up, Keisha took both tests and waited in the bathroom for the results to populate. When she looked at the tests, they were both positive! Keisha was shocked! She told Sasha first, then told Sasha's parents. Within a few weeks, Keisha was unemployed, confirmed pregnant by a doctor, and living back at home with her mother. Tyler was excited about the news! He was very happy...so happy that he proposed to Keisha over the phone after she told him the news.

CHAPTER TWO

Then Came Marriage

Everything that Keisha ever wanted was finally happening. Albeit a bit out of order, but she was happy about her baby and her pending nuptials. Once again, Keisha found herself talking to Tyler about meeting the family...and once again, he had a major issue with doing it. He wanted to avoid meeting her family for as long as he could, but Keisha's sister, Sharla, kept insisting they come over. As fate would have it, Tyler could no longer avoid meeting Keisha's family because of Sharla's plan...he had no idea where he was going on until he got to the house. He was so upset with Keisha for not telling him, but he understood why she didn't say anything. By the end of the visit, Sharla and Tyler did not see eye to eye on a lot of things and concluded that they did not like each other...AT ALL!

Sharla felt like Tyler was up to something and she didn't trust him. She thought Keisha should leave him immediately. But little did she know that they were on the verge of becoming one in holy matrimony. Keisha did not tell her family right away about the marriage because everyone was still getting news of her pregnancy. Tyler really didn't tell his family or friends either. With a baby on the way, they had so much more to think and worry about. When Keisha was about four months pregnant, Tyler left for the military. They both agreed it was the best thing to do to have security for their family. While Tyler was away, Keisha started preparing for their future life by getting things together. They discussed everything over the phone and Keisha made it happen. They planned to marry before Keisha had the baby and once Tyler reached his duty station and got settled, he would come back so they could tie the knot. They called two of their friends to be witnesses so those were the only ones they thought would be in attendance. To their surprise, Sharla and Keisha's mom showed up with gifts for Keisha and Tyler.

After several minutes of waiting, it was finally time to get the ceremony started. The pastor came in and started it off, "Dearly Beloved…" As Keisha and Tyler stood side by side, waiting to say their vows, they both started shaking. Keisha was hormonal and her emotions were everywhere. She was 8 1/2 months pregnant. Tyler was a wreck because he was terrified about being married. The entire time the pastor was conducting the ceremony, Tyler was shaking in his boots. He was so terrified! Keisha noticed how much he was shaking and tried to hold his hands and calm him down. Nevertheless, they stood there, ready to commit to one another for eternity. Keisha was dressed in black capris with a black and white stripped tunic. Her feet were swollen so she wore flip flops to complete her bridal attire. Tyler was dressed in an all-black ensemble. He wore a black t-shirt, black jeans, black boots and a black construction style coat. The ceremony was short and straight to the point. They got to the moment where they had to exchange their first kiss as husband and wife. Keisha was smiling from ear to ear, looking at Tyler. He was looking at Keisha, afraid to kiss her, but knowing that he was in too deep to back out now.

They kissed and the few attendees cheered. Everyone congratulated the newlyweds and walked out of the chapel. Keisha's mother gave her a wedding gift basket, hugged her tight and looked at her as if she would never see her again. It was the strangest look Keisha had ever seen from her mother. Her sister hugged her and congratulated her. Keisha was confused as to why her mother looked the way she did. She just brushed it off as her mom being her mom, but it came off like she was just there to be there but wasn't too happy about Keisha and Tyler getting married. It was a weird atmosphere. A few moments after the gifts were given, Keisha and Tyler went to the car. Tyler opened the door for Keisha and placed the basket in her lap. Keisha opened it and found all kinds of sweets and goodies, sparkling juice, and a card with money from her mom. Tyler and Keisha didn't have much of anything, so they appreciated the gifts very much. They used the money from the card to get a hotel room for the night. Once they checked-in, they went down the street and got dinner from the coney island. Tyler decided he wanted to see his family while he was in town and dropped Keisha back off at the hotel.

She ate most of her dinner alone in the hotel room while Tyler took her car and went to visit his family. When Keisha woke up, it was 8 in the morning and Tyler was just getting back to the room. Keisha asked if his family was happy to see him and he told her they were. She was happy that he was back and was ready to get the day started. Tyler told her they didn't have much time because his bus was leaving out around one that afternoon. Keisha wanted to spend more time with her husband while he was there, but he had other plans. Tyler was embarrassed by how much weight Keisha had gained since he last saw her. He didn't want to be seen with her in the public more than he had to. He would rather wait at the bus station for hours than to be out with her.

The more Keisha tried to spend time with him, the more he mentioned the time and how he needed to be at the bus station. Because her hormones were all over the place, she didn't think too much about Tyler being in such a rush to get back. She just figured that he didn't want to miss his bus. Keisha had no idea that her weight gain was an issue for Tyler. She knew that she had put on more weight than she wanted to, but she felt like it was just because she was pregnant. Keisha was only one month away from her induction date when they were married. Once Keisha dropped Tyler off, she went back to her mother's house. She was excited and nervous about having the baby and moving to be with Tyler real soon, but she was happy.

Once Tyler got back to base, he called Keisha and let her know he had arrived. She was so happy that he made it back safely. She asked about the bus ride and told him about her day. They talked about their plans moving forward and the birth of the baby. Keisha learned early in the pregnancy that the baby would most likely have Down Syndrome. When she initially found out, she called Tyler and cried. She was so afraid, and Tyler did his best to comfort her over the phone. They had no idea what to expect but they were going to face it together. They didn't have much of a choice because she would be born soon. Although they told their families about the baby's potential diagnosis, everyone was still so happy to meet her. Keisha was the last of her siblings to have kids, but Tyler would be the first of his siblings. They were sharing so many new things with one another, but there was something that Tyler didn't share with Keisha. He didn't tell her that his family didn't know they are married.

Tyler's family was under the impression that Tyler and Keisha were only dating, and Keisha got pregnant. The night they were married, Tyler went to visit his family. He had his ring on and took pictures and stayed with them all night long catching up and chilling. All that time that he was there, he never mentioned to his family that he and Keisha had gotten married earlier that day. The truth had to come out soon because the baby would be arriving in a few weeks and Tyler wanted to make sure that his parents met Keisha and the baby before it was time for them to move. While Keisha was extremely upset when she found out that Tyler kept the wedding a secret, she was even more upset when Tyler told her that he wouldn't be at the birth of their child. From the moment she knew the date of induction, Keisha told Tyler she wanted him to be there...and he promised her that he would be there. A few days before Keisha was to be induced, he told her that he wouldn't be able to make it and she was totally devastated. Keisha packed her bag and prepared to go have a baby. When she arrived at the hospital, she was scared and felt so alone. She checked in early in the morning and laid in bed waiting to give birth to her daughter. She was worried about everything the doctors told her about her baby, but she was also excited to meet her. Tyler's family didn't know much about what was going on with Keisha and the baby and they weren't interested in being involved with Keisha like that.

Although Tyler's family was distant from Keisha, she had a circle of support around her. Her sister, her mom, and one of her sorority sisters met Keisha at the hospital. She was so happy to have them there with her. Her induction began and she prepared to give birth. Both Keisha's mom and sister were excited to be there with her. One of the happiest people in the room was Keisha's sorority sister. She was so happy for Keisha and super excited to meet the baby! She was there throughout the entire process. She was so happy to be part of the birth. The moments between contractions were short and every breath was filled with the pressure to push. Keisha was laying on her side while her soror rubbed her back.

"Uhhhhh, Keisha...are you ok?" she asked

"Yes." Keisha responded between contractions.

"Well, I'm gonna' go get the nurse 'cause I see blood." her soror said.

As she went to get the nurse, Keisha kept breathing slowly and her mom kept her company.

"Alright...OOOHHHHH! Is everything ok in here?" asked the nurse when she walked in and saw the blood on the sheet.

"Umm hmm" Keisha replied.

"Well, there is a lot of blood on the sheets so let's go ahead and check you, ok?" the nurse asked

"Umm hmm" Keisha continued to lightly whimper as she turned on her back.

"WHOA! That's why there's blood! The baby is crowning! Call the doctor! The nurse shouted.

They told Keisha not to push for the next few contractions that were coming rapidly. They tried to break the bed down as fast as they could, but they didn't have time. There wasn't even enough time to wait for the doctor to arrive. The baby was coming faster than anyone could prepare for.

"Alright, next contraction I want you to push...the baby is almost out." Keisha grabbed the rails on the bed while bearing down and got ready to push.

"Next contraction, she'll be out", the nurse said.

The next contraction came and so did the baby! Keisha was so happy that her baby was alive and well! Her excitement didn't last long though. As soon as Heaven was born, she was rushed to the NICU for tests. Keisha was released from the hospital before Heaven, but a few days later, they were reunited. Keisha talked to Tyler every day and told him everything that was going on. Prior to the doctors releasing Heaven, they diagnosed her with Down Syndrome, but thankfully, none of the other issues they predicted were detected. Keisha and Tyler were so grateful! Keisha and Heaven went to Keisha's mom's house for a few weeks while they waited for the doctors to give the ok for Heaven to travel. Keisha was excited to move to a new city and start her new life as a military wife and mother!

Keisha had to wait almost two weeks to go to the doctor to have Heaven checked out before they could leave. Once she was cleared, Keisha and Tyler planned for them to travel. Before Keisha and Heaven left, Tyler wanted her to take Heaven to his parents' house so they could meet their grandbaby. Keisha was a bit aggravated that Tyler wanted her to do this "meet and greet" without him. Tyler kept trying to reassure Keisha that it would be cool, and that she just needed to make it happen. Tyler was living on base preparing for Keisha and Heaven to join him so he couldn't come home at the time. He was very adamant and kept insisting that Keisha take Heaven to his parents' home before they left. Keisha was nervous and afraid to go meet Tyler's family by herself. She had spoken to Tyler's mom a few times on the phone, but it was rarely pleasant.

Keisha recalled an incident in which Tyler's mom was very vocal about how they were making a huge mistake by having a baby. Another time, she told Keisha that she figured Tyler would always "do the right thing" if he ever got a girl pregnant. Although Keisha felt like she and Tyler's mother would never have a good relationship, she did feel somewhat connected to the family because she knew two of Tyler's brothers. She used to braid their hair when she was in high school, but she didn't know of Tyler at the time because he was never around.

Tyler called his parents and set up the meeting. After he spoke to his family, he called Keisha and told her where to go and what time to be there. Keisha was so nervous she talked to Heaven during the whole ride. She was uncomfortable going to meet the rest of Tyler's family without him. She felt like her mother-in-law hated her already by the way she always spoke to her on the phone. Since she was giving off such crazy vibes, Keisha had no idea what to expect from the rest of her in-laws.

She pulled into the driveway and slowly approached the house. As she walked up the stairs, she held Heaven tightly in her arms. She reached the front door and took a deep breath. With a shaking hand, she rang the doorbell and stood motionless and in fear. She waited patiently at the door for a few moments and suddenly, the door opened.

"Hi. Come on in" said a young girl who looked to be a year or so younger than Keisha.

"Thank you" Keisha said as she walked in the house.

"I'm Tyler's sister Layla"

"Nice to meet you, I'm Keisha".

"Follow me", Layla told Keisha. They walked through the house, to the back den and joined the parents.

"Hello", Keisha said.

"Hey, how you doin'?" Tyler's parents greeted her in unison.

They quickly exchanged pleasantries and focused their attentions toward the baby. Everyone wanted to see Heaven! She was a small baby with the cutest face ever. She was only two weeks old, so she slept most of the time during the introductions. Tyler's parents, Steve and Karen, were so happy to see Heaven and hold her. They didn't really talk to Keisha much because they were enamored with Heaven. They wanted to spend all day with her. As time passed, they begin to talk to Keisha more. Steve did most of the talking, as he wanted to make Keisha feel welcome. Karen joined the conversation once Layla and Lucas, the youngest son, came into the room. Keisha finally started to relax once because she recognized a familiar face. The tension in the room released and she was able to enjoy spending time with her new family. Each moment came with a revelation and the more Keisha thought things were getting better, they were actually staying the same.

When she left that night, she called Tyler to tell him how everything went. He told her to relax and that it was cool. She still didn't feel too good about how things went down. She felt like she was an unwanted houseguest who was just being tolerated for the sake of keeping the peace. Heaven was the center of attraction, and while Keisha knew that they would be excited to meet the baby, she didn't realize that she would be treated as an outcast. When she tried to explain her feelings to Tyler, he dismissed them and told her she needed to chill. It was hard for Keisha to accept how she was feeling. She didn't know how to deal with it all or who to talk to about it. She was scared and concerned about what her future was going to be like as a member of this family. Regardless of how she was feeling, she was moving to the military base with Tyler in less than a week.

Keisha still had a lot to handle before she and Heaven could move. She had to go change her name since she was married now and get a new id. Once she handled all her errands, it was time to pack and say goodbye to family and friends. Keisha didn't have a lot of her own things to take...mostly everything she had to pack was for Heaven. As it got closer to the day for them to leave, Keisha and her mother started to spend more time together. Patricia gave Keisha tips on how to keep her marriage together and reduce friction.

"Keisha, one thing I want you to remember is that the right hand don't have to let the left hand know what it's doing", Patricia said.

Keisha looked at her mother with a confused look waiting for her to elaborate.

"You don't need to tell him about everything you doin'. There are some things that you should keep to yourself. Especially money. You never know what could happen so you want to make sure you and Heaven will be ok", Patricia explained as she placed five crisp one-hundred-dollar bills in Keisha's hand.

Keisha was so thankful that her mom had blessed them with such a nice gift. She was a little thrown off by her mom telling her to keep secrets from Tyler. She heard the advice but didn't understand the point or purpose of it. Keisha felt like she should be able to tell Tyler everything. In Keisha's mind, a marriage is composed of two individuals who want to work as one to achieve goals. For the life of her, she couldn't wrap her mind around where her mom was coming from with the advice she gave. Due to their relationship history, Keisha didn't think she would get much clarity from her mom if she asked for it, so she didn't say anything. Patricia didn't really care for Tyler and honestly, neither did Keisha's sister. Regardless of what they thought about Tyler, they supported Keisha and her decision. Keisha finished packing everything up and confirmed the travel plans with her dad.

Gerald loved taking trips with Keisha but this one was very different from any trip they ever took. Keisha said all her goodbyes to her friends and family. She didn't talk to Tyler much during the last few days before the move. They were both really busy planning to be reunited and Tyler had to prepare to meet his daughter. Gerald had to get ready for his last road trip with his daughter. It was a very emotional time for everyone. Keisha was inundated with everything as the time grew closer for her and Heaven to leave. She didn't know what life would be like in a new place with new responsibilities and a new baby. She was clueless about what she was expected to do as a military wife. She didn't know what the journey would be like raising a child with special needs. She was used to living in a major city and she didn't know what Warner Robins, Georgia would be like. All the excitement shifted into uncertainty.

The only stable thing to keep Keisha grounded was knowing that she had to take care of Heaven. Keisha had to stay grounded and focused no matter what her emotions were taking her through. All her emotions settled on the morning of November 27, 2004. Gerald arrived early at Patricia's house to pick up Keisha and Heaven. It was time to take the drive from the westside of Detroit to smack dab in the middle of Georgia. Gerald loaded the truck with everything Keisha and Heaven had. Keisha hugged her mom and her sister, who arrived just in time to say goodbye. She grabbed Heaven and loaded her car seat in the truck. She wiped her tears and closed the door. She was leaving the only place she ever really knew to start life somewhere she'd never been. Gerald got in the truck and blew the horn as they pulled off. As they drove down the street Keisha's tears dried up and she started to feel the sadness drift away. It was twelve hours of growing anticipation. The ride was so peaceful. The sky got brighter as they got closer to the base. When they arrived, it was a whole new world for Keisha, Gerald, and Heaven.

Everything was gated and secured. Gerald was instructed to drive to the visitor center to wait for Tyler to come get them on the base. Keisha was keeping Tyler abreast on their arrival time so he would know when to be available. She let him know that they were at the gate waiting and he got dressed and headed up there. When he arrived, he went to the truck and opened Keisha's door to see his wife and daughter.

"Hey baby", Tyler whispered in Keisha's ear as he hugged and kissed her. Once he let Keisha go, he wanted to see Heaven.

"Heaven, here is your daddy", Keisha said when she gave Heaven to Tyler.

"She is so little. I think I'm gonna call her Tiny. Yeah. Her nickname is Tiny", Tyler said looking at his daughter.

Gerald was happy to see them reunited. Tyler gave Heaven back to Keisha and told Gerald to take his driver's license and insurance card out so they could go to the visitor center and handle the paperwork so they could unload the truck. Gerald started up the truck and followed Tyler to their new house. Keisha was so happy when they pulled up. The house was really nice. They were some of the newest houses on base. Gerald backed in and started unloading immediately. Tyler helped Gerald unload the heavy stuff from the truck. There wasn't a lot to get so it didn't take long to unload. Gerald closed the lift gate on his truck then he closed the door on the truck bed cap. Gerald went inside to use the restroom and get some water. He didn't stay more than 10 minutes.

"Alright baby, I'll see you later", Gerald called out to

Keisha. She was upstairs with Heaven changing her diaper.

"I'm coming Dad!", she yelled back.

She finished changing Heaven and asked Tyler to come down to say bye to her father. Tyler went with a reluctant disposition. They went downstairs as a family. Keisha thanked her father and hugged him. She asked him to stay for a little while, but he said he would rest on the road because he needed to get back for church Sunday morning. Gerald kissed Heaven and shook Tyler's hand before he got in his truck. Tyler had to go into work that night, so he was heading out with Gerald. Tyler led Gerald to the exit and went to work. Keisha and Heaven got settled into their new home. Tyler's schedule was difficult for Keisha to adjust to at first. She didn't know anyone but Tyler and he worked the first 10 days straight from the time Keisha and Heaven arrived.

He was working 12 hours a day for 10 days. It was brutal for Keisha. She felt isolated, confined, restricted. She didn't know what to do. She only had Heaven to spend real time with. Keisha tried to find things to do to keep her busy. Heaven was a very quiet baby. She didn't cry much, and she didn't really want much in those first few weeks. Tyler was focused on a tough case at work, and he was not really available to be there the way Keisha needed him to be. When Tyler's superior learned that Tyler had a new wife and child on base, he immediately referred Tyler to a program on base that provided support for military families and spouses especially.

After the stretch of long days, Tyler finally had a break and was able to spend time with Keisha at home. He told her about the program and encouraged her to check into it. Tyler and Keisha didn't have much furniture for the first few weeks due to Tyler's schedule. Tyler's first day off he invited a few of his friends over to play video games. It was a knock at the door and Tyler went to answer it. Keisha heard the commotion as they entered and made their way upstairs. They all piled into the bedroom where Keisha and Heaven were.

"Hey guys, this is my wife Keisha and my daughter Heaven. Keisha, these the fellas. Franklin, Johnson, and Russell." Tyler said.

They all greeted one another and then the guys went to the foot of the bed and the floor and started playing the game. Keisha was happy to have people around, but she was extremely uncomfortable at the same time. The more Tyler invited his friends over and included Keisha and Heaven in with the guys, the more it made Keisha feel weird. She was feeling disconnected from her friends, family, and her sense of normality. There were a lot of adjustments that Keisha had to make. She appreciated being included but she wanted to have her own friends and support. Keisha remembered the program that Tyler told her about when she moved there. She called the number and found out what she needed to do to get involved.

She learned that they had meetings once a month and signed up to attend the next meeting. Shortly after she signed up, Tyler told Keisha that they were having a guest for dinner. His friend Johnson and his fiancé were coming to dinner. Keisha was excited and skeptical at the same time. She was looking forward to meeting new people but was cautious about befriending women. Keisha had some bad experiences with her female friends and that made her question all females. It seemed that Johnson's fiancé was a bit skeptical too.

It was a cool dinner and they slowly started getting to know one another. Keisha told Brenda about the spouse meeting and invited her to join. They went to the meeting and met some other spouses from the same squadron.

It was comforting for both Keisha and Brenda. They felt like they had a home away from home with women who understood. It was easy for them to connect with the women in the group. Everyone was vulnerable very early in the meeting, but guards were dropped immediately. They had an unbreakable bond by the end of the dinner. Keisha was thankful to have friends and an outlet. A few months later, Brenda, Keisha, and another one of the wives were all pregnant at the same time. Keisha and Brenda were so excited to go through this journey together. They had become really close since the meeting. Keisha was especially happy because this pregnancy was carefully planned after a devastating miscarriage. Brenda was excited because this was her first child. The pregnancies flew by so fast for both of them.

Before they knew it, they were having a baby shower and then a few weeks later, they had bouncing baby boys. Life was moving so fast, but Keisha and Brenda made the most of it. They were happy to have one another in the midst of a strange place and new life. Brenda and Johnson asked Keisha and Tyler to be the godparents of their son. It was a great honor for them to be thought of in that way. They humbly accepted and were thrilled about being chosen. Since Keisha and Tyler now had two kids, they were able to move into a larger house on base. Everything was improving in their life. Tyler made rank and things were good. Then things changed again. The relationship got even more rocky, and Keisha and Tyler were at odds. In the middle of the hostility, Tyler had to leave for deployment training.

CHAPTER THREE

Meeting His Needs

Keisha was devastated to learn that she and the kids would be alone while Tyler was away. However, all of that quickly changed. While Tyler was away, Keisha's aunt died. Once the arrangements were made, the family began making travel plans to attend the funeral. When Patricia called and told Keisha that her aunt had died, she told her she would pay for their tickets home. Patricia knew that Keisha wanted to attend the funeral but couldn't afford it on her own. Patricia's sister saved Keisha's life when she was younger, and they had a special relationship. Keisha was really hurt to hear about her aunt's passing but thankful that her mom was making sure she could be there. Keisha told Tyler about her aunt, and he shared his condolences. Her flight left a few hours before Tyler's flight landed back home from training. Tyler didn't like that. When he spoke to Keisha, he let her know how he felt.

"Hello", Keisha said.

"Where are you?" Tyler asked acting as if he didn't know.

"I'm in Detroit Tyler. I told you I was coming home."

"What are you up there for? You should be here with me! I just got home and I'm hungry." Tyler explained.

Keisha paused for a few moments before she responded,

"Tyler, I told you I was coming up here for my aunt's funeral. There is food in the fridge, and you know how to cook. What are you tripping on?"

"It's Thanksgiving and you should be here cooking me something to eat. Your aunt is already dead. She is not going to miss you if you leave and come back here." Tyler told Keisha.

"Are you serious?" Keisha asked with utter disbelief.

"I'm divorcing you if you don't come back home!" Tyler threatened Keisha.

"No Tyler! Don't do this! What is wrong with you? Why are you saying that?" Keisha cried out.

"So, are you coming home?"

"Yes Tyler. After the funeral. I'll be home Sunday."

"No Keisha, come home today or I'm divorcing you!"

"Tyler, stop throwing that threat around. That's not funny."

"I'm serious Keisha! Come home or I'm shipping your stuff up there! You don't have to come back!"

"Ok Tyler." Keisha said calmly.

"What you mean ok? You coming home?"

"No. You can ship my stuff up here." Keisha said with a sound of defeat that weighed her voice down.

Tyler hung up the phone and within 20 minutes, he disconnected the service on Keisha's phone. She talked to a few members of her family about getting her and the kids' things and getting a new phone. Some agreed to help her, and some encouraged her to go back and make amends with her husband. The next day, Keisha called Tyler from her new number and let him know she would come get their things. Tyler burst into tears and begged Keisha to forgive him. He told her he was stressed about training and getting deployed and just wanted his wife there with him. Keisha accepted his explanation and went home Sunday as planned. When they arrived to the airport, Tyler was there beaming with joy. Keisha was silent most of the ninety-minute drive home. Tyler talked a lot. When they arrived home, Tyler treated Keisha like a queen.

As she moved about the house, she was inundated with notes of gratitude, romance, and appreciation from Tyler. He made sure that she didn't want for anything. A month later, Tyler left for his deployment. The deployment was hard on both of them. It was a four-month deployment due to the location. They couldn't really talk on the phone much, so they emailed one another. Keisha was trying to keep everything together while Tyler was in a foreign country attempting to stay out of danger. Tyler was concerned about the kids forgetting him because they were so young. Keisha just wanted Tyler to make it home safely. After several months, they reached the end of the deployment and Tyler and his unit were headed home. Keisha was so happy! Tyler came home and Keisha showed him how much she missed him. Tyler was given two weeks off after a month of being home. Before the end of the first two week, Keisha and Tyler were suddenly on the brink of breaking up again. They couldn't agree on anything. Every little thing became a big issue. Tyler didn't trust Keisha. Keisha didn't understand what was going on.

Then boom...they found out they are having another baby! Keisha didn't want to bring another child into this rollercoaster life. Tyler was happy because he wanted more kids anyway. He didn't show any concern for the relationship. He only showed concern for things that were important to him. When Tyler's family needed something, they called him, and he sent it. When Keisha and the kids needed things, Tyler wanted to see receipts for anything she had to spend money on. He would ask for proof that certain things were needed like diapers, wipes, and cleaning supplies.

When Keisha would go to the store to get items, Tyler would randomly ask to smell her underwear when she returned to make sure she wasn't cheating while she was out. More and more, the relationship became one-sided. Tyler treated Keisha more like an employee than his wife. Their life was completely different from what she imagined. In an effort to keep up the facade, Keisha went back to Detroit with Tyler for his two weeks off after the deployment. Tyler and Keisha did not want to tell anyone they were expecting just yet, but it came out while they were at Tyler's parent's house. Most of Tyler's family was excited for the most part, but for some reason, Tyler's mom had a disapproving tone whenever she spoke to Keisha about her children.

Keisha could not understand why her mother-in-law's had issues with her and Tyler having kids. In spite of what his mother said, Keisha stayed calm, respectful, and hidden most of the time they were there. One night after dinner, Tyler disappeared outside. His parents asked where he was after about 30 minutes, so Keisha went outside to look for him. When she stepped outside all she could see was a car sitting in the driveway with the parking lights on. She walked towards the car and just before she reached the hood, the lights came on and the door opened.

Tyler hopped out from the passenger side of the car, calling Keisha's name. Keisha's eyes adjusted and saw Tyler standing outside of the car with the door open. When he opened the door, the interior lights came on in the car. Tyler told Keisha to go back inside. Keisha was hurt. She couldn't believe that he was sitting outside all this time with another woman! She shook off the shock of the moment and did what Tyler said...she went back inside. Tyler came in about 20 minutes later. Keisha went to the back room where they were staying. Tyler came in and went straight into the front room with his family to avoid Keisha. He waited about an hour before he went to the room with Keisha.

"Tyler who was that?" Keisha asked immediately.

"A friend Keisha." Tyler responded as if he was annoyed by the question.

"So why didn't you invite her in so she could meet us if she is a friend?" Keisha inquired.

"She didn't need to meet y'all!" Tyler said as to end the conversation.

Keisha dropped her head and thought about how close they were to ending their marriage and having another baby. She could not wrap her mind around what had just happened. Tyler was not concerned about how Keisha was feeling. He was only worried about himself and what he wanted. He left the room and didn't communicate or spend time with Keisha for the rest of the trip. When she wanted to go out of the house, he would tell her to find a sitter for the kids and leave. Tyler began to treat Keisha even worse than before. He focused more on making her suffer than making her happy. The last few days of the trip mellowed out and when it was time to leave, the family shared hugs and well wishes as Keisha and Tyler loaded the truck. For Keisha, she was simply going through the motions. She felt a strong, disapproving vibe from her mother-in-law and sister-in-law...stronger than in past visits. For Tyler, this trip was different. He was enjoying being with his family and doing what he wanted, when he wanted, how he wanted, without regard for how it would affect others. The drive home was rather quiet.

Everyone slept most of the ride while Keisha drove. When they returned home, it was back to the normal schedule. Keisha wasn't working but wanted to do something productive with her time. She helped Tyler complete his real estate courses and thought about going back to school. She talked to Tyler about it, and he encouraged her to do it. He did tell Keisha that she had to use their joint bank account for her refund checks from school. Although they were not in the best place, Keisha agreed. She thought she would have a degree at the end and have a great career that would balance things back out. She started the process of applying for school. Tyler completed his real estate program but was not able to take the test. Right after he completed the last course, he was notified that he was being deployed again. When he told Keisha, it was like all their problems disappeared and they were one again. They were devastated. Tyler had to leave for training eight days after he learned of the deployment. Tyler was worried about Keisha being pregnant and alone. He encouraged her to find a job she could do from home. Keisha liked the idea of that because she would still be able to do her schoolwork if she worked from home.

One of Keisha's friends told her about in-home day care as a business and how lucrative it is. She investigated it and went to the next information class that was available. Before they knew it, it was time for Tyler to leave for his deployment. It was a weird time for them. Nevertheless, they knew what they had to do. Tyler wiped Keisha's tears away and they kissed good-bye. Tyler loaded up on the bus with his fellow soldiers. Keisha stood on the sidewalk with their children until the bus pulled away. Once the buses left, Keisha packed up the kids and went home. A few weeks after Tyler left, Keisha received her certification to operate her in-home day care. She was still waiting on her transcripts from her previous school to be sent to the new school. She was happy to have the daycare going while she was waiting and Tyler was away. Things were going well for the first few months. Keisha's business was doing well, the kids were doing good, and Tyler was safe. Although he was safe, he was miserable.

"Hello" Keisha said as she answered her phone.

"Hey baby" Tyler said after a slight delay from the other end.

"Hi Honey! How are you?" Keisha asked with pure concern and excitement.

"I'm ready to come home baby. I can't take this." Tyler said fighting back tears.

"I know. We are ready for you to be home.", she said in an attempt to comfort him.

"No. I NEED to come home! I need YOU to help me get home early!" he shouted.

Keisha heard the despair and pain in his voice and told him she would come up with something. He told her that a friend was killed in action near his location. He was watching horrendous acts take place constantly. He had to endure every moment of it because it was all part of his job. Tyler didn't reveal how heavy his friend's death was on him. Nor did he share his true feelings about Keisha. He ended the call and Keisha began to worry. She had to come up with a plan to get Tyler home early. She asked some of the other wives what she could do, and they helped her pull it off. Within weeks, Tyler was scheduled to fly home. He arrived back two months earlier than everyone he was deployed with. When he came home, things changed very quickly. The baby was due in a couple of weeks after he came home. Their home life was tense. Tyler spent a lot of time away from home when Keisha was supposed to be on bed rest. Tyler started hanging out with his friends, who were still on base, almost every night until the day Keisha's water broke.

"Tyler!" Keisha yelled upstairs.

"What?!?" He yelled back.

"Bring a towel down please, my water just broke." she told him as he leaned over the stairs looking down at her.

"Are you sure? Or did you just pee on yourself and you don't wanna' tell me?" Tyler joked.

"Bring a towel please. I did not pee on myself. I'm going to the car while you get the kids, " she said with an unbothered tone as she walked outside.

Tyler took his time bringing a towel and the kids downstairs. He did what he wanted and how he wanted. He felt like there was no need to rush because it's just going to take all day to have the baby anyway. He moved slowly loading up the car, he drove slowly to the hospital, and he didn't make any urgent moves when they arrived. Once they got Keisha checked in, they learned that there was meconium in the fluid, which could pose a major threat to the baby.

Keisha remained calm and Tyler was just as indifferent as he was when they arrived. Keisha was concerned but remained calm. She knew she had to keep it all together. Time continued to pass with no baby being born. Tyler laid on the hospital couch in the delivery room waiting room, waiting for something to happen. Keisha hid her disdain with Tyler by practicing her breathing techniques. A little later, the nurse came in and talked to Keisha about getting an epidural to help the dilation go a little better. Hours later, the nurse came in to check Keisha again to see if she had dilated more since her last visit.

"Keisha, it seems like you are stuck at 7cm and it has been about 12 hours since your water broke. We are at the point where we need to bring the doctor in to prep for a c-section", the nurse told Keisha

"Ok", Keisha said with a somber response.

Within moments, things shifted swiftly. The nurse came back into the room and checked Keisha once again.

"Well, Keisha. I have good news", she said.

"What?" Keisha responded with pain and concern.

"You're completely dilated. It's time to push. We are gonna get the doctor in here and you'll start pushing", she said.

Keisha kept breathing and thinking about the experience. Although the room quickly filled with people, Keisha felt completely alone. Tyler's nap was interrupted when the wave of people entered. He quickly sat up on the couch, watching the staff get Keisha ready to deliver. He sat there until they called him over to help hold Keisha's legs to push.

"Alright Keisha, this should be the last few pushes and you'll have a baby", the nurse said. Within moments, Keisha gave birth to a beautiful baby girl.

When they got home, it was a whole new life for Tyler, Keisha, and their family. Although Keisha did not like the idea of having another child, she was overwhelmed with joy when she met the baby. Tyler seemed extremely happy with the birth of the new baby. He was so pleased to have what he viewed as a "perfect baby". She was everything he wanted Heaven and their son to be. She was immediately his favorite. The joy of the new baby quickly wore off once they were home and Tyler went back to work. Tyler returned to his old self and Keisha was now a mom of three. It was evident that Tyler was eager to have the baby but could care less about taking care of anything associated with parenting. Keisha realized she was in this alone.

Tyler began to spend more and more time away from the house, hanging out with his friends. Keisha spent most of her time just trying to find herself again. She talked to Tyler and let him know how she was feeling. He encouraged her to go back to school and finish working towards her degree. Keisha was so excited to do something for herself, she jumped in headfirst. As soon as she jumped, Tyler started tripping again.

"WHAT?!" Tyler responded to Keisha, after she interrupted his video game.

"I need to go to the store", Keisha told him.

"Well, you better take them with you cause I'm busy", he explained.

Keisha dropped her head, rolled her eyes, and got the kids ready to go to the store. "What are you buying now?" Tyler asked.

"The kids need diapers, we need toilet paper, and I want to get laundry detergent", she told him.

"Well make sure you not getting the name brand, expensive shit!" he instructed. Keisha shook her head in agreeance. "You hear what I said?" Tyler asked as he walked up to Keisha and stood in front of her.

"Yes Tyler, I shook my head yes", she explained.

"I wasn't looking at you, so you need to make sure you answer me out loud", Tyler scolded Keisha.

"Whatever Tyler", Keisha said.

For months, their relationship continued in the same manner as this encounter. Tyler instructed and Keisha reluctantly followed along. Tyler became more and more self-centered in his actions and interactions with his family. He and Keisha continued to grow further and further apart. This was a hard pill to swallow for Keisha. She felt like her marriage was falling apart right in front of her eyes and there was nothing she could do about it. The more Tyler pulled away, the more Keisha tried to keep him connected to the children. She knew at this point that he was no longer interested in being her husband.

Tyler wanted Keisha to stop attempting to explain her side, her feelings, her emotions, and any other concerns. He didn't care about any of that. He wasn't concerned about his wife or kids...he just wanted to do whatever he wanted and felt Keisha should remain silent. He stopped listening to Keisha anytime she spoke. He began to ignore her in a way that was evident to those who were around them. It was a strange relationship on the outside looking in. Keisha was aware that she needed to get out but didn't have a clue on how to do it. She did not have money, support, or a plan. She felt like going back to school and earning her degree would put her in position to leave Tyler, but she had no idea what the journey would look like. She just didn't care anymore. Her focus was just going through the motions so that she could get her degree and take care of her kids.

Tyler didn't care about what Keisha was doing outside of him as long as she followed his orders. The disrespect led to multiple altercations, until finally, it happened. Tyler pushed Keisha and made her hit the wall. He teased her about her past and taunted her until she reacted by yelling at him. Tyler thought that was funny and continued. He poked and pushed Keisha until she pushed back, and they began tussling. It was a quick altercation, but the damage had already commenced.

CHAPTER FOUR

Back To School

Keisha had everything in place for her return to school. Just when she was about to register for classes, she was notified that her balance from the first university was carrying over and would need to be paid before she could enroll. Keisha felt like she was once again stuck. With all the turmoil between her and Tyler, she thought there was no way she would be able to have a conversation with him about the situation. However, after a few weeks, Tyler brought the conversation to Keisha.

"What's going on with your school shit?" he asked.

"I have to pay the balance before I can register", she told him.

"So, what's the balance?" he asked.

"Forty-five hundred dollars", she said.

"Well let's get a loan or something to pay it off so you can register", Tyler told Keisha.

"Ok", she said with surprise and hesitancy.

She was SO caught off guard that Tyler wanted to help her after everything that was going on. To her surprise, Tyler was actually acting as if he was truly invested in Keisha's success. It was a welcome change as far as Keisha was concerned. However, she knew not to get too excited about Tyler's attitude adjustment. Tyler didn't really acknowledge the change in attitude or behavior. As time progressed. they learned that Keisha was ineligible for a loan because she was unemployed. Keisha decided to look for ways to earn money online from home so that she could look better to lenders. Keisha was having little to no success finding lucrative work from home opportunities. Keisha contacted one of her spouse friends and told them what was going on. They gave her info about a job on the military base that she might qualify for.

Keisha checked into it and found out that it was a delivery driver position on base. She thought this could be a great chance to earn money while they figured out the loan situation. Tyler seemed indifferent about it. He didn't show any interest in Keisha working again but liked the idea of having more money coming in. For that reason, Tyler didn't object. Although Tyler was not keen on Keisha having full independence, he enjoyed watching her get excited about stuff. Keisha got the job and ending up being one of the most requested delivery drivers on base. Tyler didn't like all the attention she was getting so he told her to quit. When she came home after her last day of work, Tyler told her that he was approved for a loan to cover the balance so Keisha could register for classes.

Keisha didn't know how to feel about this. She was confused. She didn't ask questions, but instead kept going through the motions, looking forward to a real change. Tyler went out a few days later and completed the process to get the loan. He knew that this would help Keisha pay off her old balance and allow her to register for classes. He also knew that this would keep Keisha busy. He didn't want her to have extra time that would keep her away from home. Keisha was excited and grateful that Tyler was willing to help her. Tyler came home with the check and told Keisha to deposit it into the account and get everything set up. As usual, she followed his instructions. The check cleared, and Keisha had the school set up the payment so that she could work towards completing her degree. This was a goal that Keisha wanted to accomplish before getting married or having kids. She wanted to be able to provide a stable life for herself and subsequently her family. Now she had the opportunity!

"Did you get the balance paid yet?" Tyler asked a few days after giving Keisha the check.

"Yes, they are processing it now at the school", Keisha told him.

"When you registering for classes then?" Tyler asked.

"As soon as the balance is cleared and my transcript is sent over to the new school, I'll be able to register", Keisha replied.

"Then how long will it take you to finish once you get started?" He inquired.

"I only have about 9 classes left to take so maybe a year and a half", she responded with uncertainty.

She thought Tyler was asking a lot of questions that she already answered. It was a bit weird, but she just kept answering his questions. Unbeknownst to her, Tyler was trying to decide if he wanted to continue his military career or if he wanted to venture off into something new.

"So can you help me with my work if I register for these classes?" Tyler asked.

"What?" Keisha responded with distinct confusion in her voice.

"I'm thinking about starting these real estate classes before I get out", Tyler explained.

Keisha looked confused about why Tyler was asking her to help him with his classes when she would be taking classes herself.

"Tyler, you do realize I'll be in school as well, right?" she asked looking for clarity.

"Yeah, I know. It's not like you'll be doing everything for me. You just gone be helping me a little bit", he justified.

Keisha attempted to explain that she would be doing her work, being a mom and a wife, keeping the house together, and helping him with his needs. Tyler couldn't grasp where Keisha was coming from. He felt like he wasn't asking much of her. He viewed himself as a great husband, a good father, and a decent man overall. He could not understand why she was overreacting to him asking for her help. As far as he was concerned, what she was doing wasn't really that important anyway. Her focus should be keeping him happy and making sure he completed his courses since he was the sole provider for the family. Tyler explained how important this was to him and their family. He told Keisha he needed her, and she finally agreed to help him. The next month, everything came through for Keisha and she was finally back to school. She took four classes the first quarter because she was excited to be back and eager to be done. Keisha was rocking those classes out, just as she always did.

Tyler was happy she was doing so well. Near the end of her first quarter, Tyler started his program. Around the same time, Keisha also received a refund from her school. Reluctantly, she told Tyler about it. She didn't want to tell him because she wanted to be able to save it but she told him because she felt like she was obligated as a wife. Tyler was super excited when Keisha told him about the refund check. He immediately started making plans for the money.

"Hell yeah! That's wass'up! Now I can add those running boards to the truck and do a few more upgrades to my car", he said.

Keisha's face displayed her disdain but her back was to Tyler when he said it, so he didn't see it.

"Do what?" she asked with her back still to Tyler.

"Get some running boards and do some upgrades to my car", he repeated.

"I wanted to save that money since it's from my loan. I want to use it for emergencies only and use it to pay off my loans if we don't need it", Keisha explained.

"Nawh', we ain't doing that. We gone spend all these refund checks how I want to spend them", he told her. "If it wasn't for me, you wouldn't have been back in school, so you owe me", he continued.

Keisha just listened and remained silent. She didn't want to argue or fight about it. She just let it be. In all honesty, Keisha felt like her only option was to stay quiet, avoid confrontation, finish school, get a good job, and leave. Tyler kept money available to help his family and wanted to use what came from the refund checks to feed his desires but wouldn't even give Keisha a monthly allowance to keep money in her pocket. She hated the feeling this gave her. She wanted to leave so bad, but she knew she couldn't. It was so hard for her to stay positive and focused on her goals. Tyler didn't feel as if he was doing anything wrong. After all, he was the one who got the loan to pay off the school balance. He was the one working so that Keisha could stay home and raise the children. He was the one who was able to purchase the house and cars. He was making all the money and should have things how he wanted them.

Since he was providing so much for Keisha, she should be pleased and more than willing to accommodate whatever his needs were. Tyler felt entitled to any and everything that Keisha received. He also felt like whatever he earned was for him and that he could do what he wanted with it. The demand of the real estate courses began to overwhelm Tyler and he depended on Keisha more and more to help him complete them. Keisha helped him stay ahead in his courses. She also worked hard to stay ahead in her own courses as well. The entire time she was also picking up the slack in other areas where Tyler was falling short. She was slowly slipping into a person she could not recognize. Nevertheless, she knew she had to keep going.

Keisha knew her children deserved more. and she had to fight through what she was feeling to get to the level she wanted and needed to be at. Tyler had no idea that Keisha felt trapped...he just knew that he wanted her to do what he wanted her to do. By the start of the second quarter, Keisha was doing great in her classes and had successfully gotten Tyler through the first set of lessons and written exams. When it was time to start his next set of lessons, Tyler learned that he would be getting deployed again. This deployment was coming at a time when their relationship was at its rockiest. Neither of them knew what to expect this time around. Both of them were looking forward to the break from each another. It was bittersweet for Keisha because she knew she would be completely alone. It was hard to accept being alone with three children and no support.

As usual, she knew she just had to keep going. There was no training this time, just a straight deployment. Tyler was scheduled to leave two weeks after he was notified of the deployment. Keisha had everything set up from the last deployment, so it was a quick and easy transition. She was able to take a break from helping Tyler complete his work since he would be gone. Although she didn't really want to be alone, she was grateful to have a break from him. The length of the deployment was supposed to be between four and six months. Tyler had to do the full deployment this time since there would be no way to get him home early. He was concerned about going away this time. He was going to a war zone on this deployment, and he was terrified of not coming back home. Keisha did not know the extent of danger Tyler would face. The time came for Tyler to leave.

It was a different departure than the ones before. It was silent and distant. The children didn't really know what was going on. They just saw their dad leave with his coworkers. Keisha watched them pull away with a slight sense of relief. She was happy that she didn't have to deal with his demands for the next few months. Their communication dwindled quickly after Tyler left. Since he was going to a war zone, he wouldn't be able to contact Keisha very much at all. and she didn't mind one bit. She was ready to get her degree finished and move on with her life. Keisha worked diligently to stay on track with her courses. It was a lot of work to be a single parent, of sorts, and a full-time student. She felt like all she had were her kids and school. She was so ready to be done that she kept taking the maximum number of classes to speed up the process.

Weeks passed quickly and Keisha grew weary. The children were growing more and more demanding. Although Tyler was overseas, he was still very much in control of the money. Keisha was limited on what she could pull out of the account. Not because Tyler put restrictions on the card but because she was afraid of how he would react if he did. Instead of tampering with the account, she just used her next refund check. Since Tyler couldn't communicate much with her, he couldn't check on what money she was getting and what she was doing with it. She tried to save as much of the check as she could, but she had to dip into it since she could only take money off the card to pay bills. She also dipped into the money to celebrate when she completed her courses.

She finally completed her degree and although she wasn't able to attend her actual graduation ceremony, she decided to throw herself a graduation party. Shortly after, she started filling out applications. She was so excited to start looking for a job so she could work in her field. But soon, her excitement wore off because she could not secure a job in her field. She was unsure why she wasn't getting any responses from all the applications she submitted. It was very frustrating for her to try over and over again just to be overlooked. Before she knew it, the time had come for the deployment to end. Keisha had no idea what things were gonna be like when Tyler got home.

CHAPTER FIVE

Never the Same

Tensions were still high when Tyler returned. It felt like they were strangers living in the same space. Keisha was still looking for a job in her field. She had been contacted for a few interviews and even did placement testing, but she didn't receive any employment offers. It seemed like things were just going...not in a particular direction, but just moving. It was as if Tyler was a completely different person when he returned. Anytime Keisha tried to talk to Tyler, the conversation always went left. One day in particular, Tyler decided to discuss a financial dilemma with Keisha to get her insight.

"So, my brother needs money to pay for an abortion for this girl he got pregnant. He called me and asked for the money, but I wanted to talk to you about it first." Tyler rambled to Keisha.

"Well...honestly, I don't think we should get involved in their situation. It doesn't make sense for you to pay for their abortion. Especially when that money could be used for something in this house." Keisha explained.

Instantly Tyler responded, "Well I'm giving him the money!"

"Ok. So why did you talk to me about it if you're just going to ignore what I say?" Keisha questioned.

"I thought you would understand...that's why! I didn't ask for your advice." He told her. "If you want to have any input on what I do with MY money, you need to have some INCOME. Until then, I really don't give a fuck how you feel about shit!" Tyler continued.

Keisha felt like she had been slapped across the face and punched in the stomach. She was devastated by what Tyler said and that he could even fix his lips to say such harsh words to her. She was speechless! At that point, the conversation ended. Keisha's determination to find a job was stronger than ever after that. She put in more applications and even looked into getting a second degree to make her more appealing in the job market. She didn't know what to do, but she knew she had to do something.

After deployments, Tyler and Keisha usually take the kids back to their hometown to visit family, but this time, Tyler decided to go alone. Keisha didn't really think anything of it. She was actually relieved. It was always so stressful for her to go home with Tyler. She felt like an outcast when she was around his family. It was as if she was tolerated because she was Tyler's wife. Keisha hated being mistreated by her in-laws. She wanted to be accepted by them but couldn't keep fighting for their love when her own husband didn't make her feel loved and supported. She didn't like the way Tyler's mom always dismissed her. More and more, Keisha wanted to just walk away from the marriage. When Tyler got ready to leave, he decided to take their son with him. Keisha didn't want to let him go but she was grateful that Tyler wanted to take him anywhere.

Tyler didn't stay gone very long this visit. When he returned, there seemed to be a different mood shift. Keisha couldn't really pinpoint what the shift was. Tyler had a crazy experience while he was deployed. When he came back, he was different. His outlook was different. His desires were different. His expectations were different. Tyler spoke to Keisha more and engaged with her more than he had in the past year.

"Keisha, I'm about to run to the mall with the homies. Imma take the boy with me." Tyler told Keisha.

She was shocked, but she got their son dressed and ready to go. Tyler left with their son and a couple of his friends. Keisha continued doing her usual routine with the girls at home. She was in the back room getting the girls dressed after their bath when their son walked in and called Keisha. She didn't know why he was calling her, but she thought something was wrong, so she gestured for him to come closer to check him out. He walked towards her and so did a cute, new puppy. It was the same puppy Keisha asked Tyler for a few days prior while they were in the pet store. She was so happy to see the puppy she screamed with excitement.

"Oh my gosh! You got the puppy!" she shouted as Tyler turned the corner and entered the room.

Tyler stood there and smiled at Keisha and before he knew it, she was on her feet, hugging him. They seemed to be in a really good place, like they were moving closer to one another. They talked about their relationship and decided to commit to one another once again. They agreed to talk to each other and not at one another. They also elected to be a one income family since Tyler was still in the military. Things were working out so well. The rough part of the marriage was behind them, and they were excited to move forward. Keisha and Tyler hosted a couple's game night and invited their friends. Keisha loved hosting so she went all out in preparations.

She planned and cooked an elaborate snack buffet and added some cool decorations to the house before everyone arrived. It was a beautiful night and for Keisha and Tyler, it felt like a celebration of their new beginning. For the next few weeks, things seemed to get better and better. It was the home lift that Keisha had been waiting for. It was closer to the type of relationship she imagined they would have. When she spoke to her friends, they told her they could see a change and even asked Keisha what she did to get Tyler to change. What was funny to Keisha was that she couldn't figure out exactly what she had done. Their relationship had done a complete 180 and although she was grateful, she could not understand what made Tyler change. Keisha didn't have to wait for too long to find out the answer to her question. On Tyler's next day off, Keisha started the conversation.

"Hey Tyler, can I talk to you for a minute?" she asked.

"What's up Keisha?" he paused then turned towards her to answer.

"I'm glad we're in such a wonderful place in our relationship. I just wanted to ask you, what do I need to do to keep us here?" she looked up at Tyler with pure submission in her eyes.

"I mean...you good. Ain't nothing I can tell you to do." he answered and walked away.

In that moment, Keisha knew that what she saw was not reality. A week later, Tyler told Keisha he had made rank and his subordinates wanted to take him out to celebrate the upcoming weekend. Keisha was completely shocked! She had no idea Tyler was even testing to rank up. Nonetheless, she congratulated him and mentioned doing something to celebrate with him, but he declined. The weekend came and everyone showed up at Keisha and Tyler's house to carpool for the night. Tyler introduced Keisha to everyone, and they left. Keisha did not typically wait up for Tyler when he went out and this time was no different.

However, no matter how hard she tried, she couldn't sleep. Before she knew it, it was 6 o'clock in the morning and she had been up all night. Around 6:40 in the morning, she finally dozed off. She was startled out of her sleep shortly after by Tyler opening the garage door and stumbling into the house. When she realized it was him, she went back to sleep. Tyler didn't let that last long before he woke her up requesting breakfast and a shoulder massage. Keisha was absolutely appalled. She had no words, no energy, and no peace. Due to how she was feeling, she refused. Tyler couldn't understand why she wouldn't fill his request.

"Come on Keish." he asked as he undressed. Keisha still refused.

"You were out all night, came home after 6 in the morning and you want me to hop up, cook you breakfast, and rub your shoulders? I'm out on that!" she explained.

Tyler immediately reacted with anger and disgust. "What you mean, you out on that?!?" he questioned.

"I'm not doing this Tyler." Keisha sighed as she walked out the bedroom.

In that moment, Tyler decided to let it go and just lay down. Keisha was so frustrated she couldn't sleep so she got the kids up and started her day. By the time Keisha laid the kids down for a nap in the afternoon, she was able to take a nap as well. Tyler woke up before his family and made enough noise to make sure he wouldn't be the only person up for much longer. To say that Keisha was annoyed was an understatement! She could not believe he asked her to do all of that after he stayed out all night with his friends then had the nerve to wake up the entire house! Keisha felt so disrespected and aggravated. She was angered by Tyler having any regard for them getting some rest. After she calmed the kids down, she fed them and went to talk to Tyler. As soon as she walked in the room, she saw Tyler on the phone.

She couldn't hear the full conversation, but she could hear Tyler's responses. From what she could make out, it seemed like Tyler was dealing with a serious situation, so she calmed down and waited for him to get off the phone. When Tyler turned around and saw Keisha standing there, he changed his posture and started using a different language. Keisha got confused. Yet and still, she waited. Tyler kept talking as one of the kids came to get Keisha. She left to clean up after them and get them situated so she could go back and talk to Tyler. When she returned to the bedroom, he was off the phone standing at the dresser waiting for Keisha to come back.

"What's up?" he asked.

"Is everything ok?" Keisha asked with concern.

"Yeah. I had to deal with a situation involving one of my female troops. She was talking about killing herself cause her boyfriend broke up with her." he explained.

"So, what did you tell her?" Keisha asked.

"I mean, I just told her not to worry about it and focus on herself." Tyler answered quickly.

"Which one of your troops is this?" Keisha asked.

"Maria. You met her last night when everybody came over...before we went out." he explained.

Keisha just stood there and looked at him. Nothing made sense to her anymore. Keisha felt like she couldn't believe anything Tyler was saying. One moment everything is going great and the next moment, there was an avalanche of crazy events. Tyler was going out more frequently and spending insane amounts of time on his phone. Keisha could feel the shift and she was slowly being drained of all she had left. A few weeks later, Tyler told Keisha she needed to go get an STD test. She agreed without question or hesitation. Tyler was infuriated.

"What the fuck?! YOU DON'T EVEN CARE?!?" Tyler yelled.

"What are you talking about Tyler?" she asked in a monotone voice.

"You just don't care at all that I said you need to get tested! You ain't ask what happened or nothing!" He exclaimed.

"Ok. What happened Tyler?" Keisha asked reluctantly.

"Me and Johnson went to the strip club a couple nights ago. He got me a dance and then the dancer took me to a V.I.P room." he told Keisha.

"Ok. I actually already took a test. I'm good so...." she replied.

"Why don't you care Keisha? Like, you just cool with it?" Tyler asked, full of confusion.

"No. You are a grown ass man making decisions. I can't control what you do and I'm not about to waste time getting mad about YOUR choices." she explained.

They went back and forth for about twenty minutes and then Tyler reveals to Keisha some heavy truth.

"Well, I ain't changing. This is me and this is who I am. If you don't like it, you can leave! I'm gone be me and that's just that!"

Keisha simply responded, "Ok" and walked away.

CHAPTER SIX

Pay for It

The next week was crazy for Tyler and Keisha. They barely spoke to one another, and the tension was heavy. It was like they were "just" roommates. The communication only existed when it came to business and financial matters. Keisha knew she couldn't continue in the relationship the way it was. She thought things would change and stay good after the last time they reconciled. Keisha was hopeful for the success of their marriage. She gave all she had and still found herself in a tense situation. It was a hard pill to swallow but she had no choice. Keisha and Tyler could not recover this time. His STD scare was the final straw. Too much damage had been done and now there was no turning back.

Keisha and Tyler were finally able to speak without arguing and they both decided that the marriage was over. Since there was no chance that they would reconcile, they needed to split amicably for the sake of the children. Tyler seemed relieved...Keisha seemed numb to it all but was still going through the motions. Once they agreed to split, they discussed exactly that that would look like.

"Well, my homeboy got a room at his house that I can rent so I'm just gone move over there while we get everything worked out." Tyler told Keisha.

"Alright, that's cool. When are you moving?" she asked.

"I'll be leaving in a few days." Tyler responded.

Before Tyler moved out, he told Keisha to look into the divorce process and find out what they needed to do. She did just that and gave Tyler the information she found. They proceeded to move forward without legal counsel per Tyler's request. The two of them went to the local bank and notarized the documents for their Pro Se divorce. By the time correspondence came back from the court, Tyler was living with his friend. He came by the house a few times to check on Keisha and to follow up on the response from the court. Keisha waited to tell Tyler that the court rejected their paperwork until she found a lawyer.

When Tyler learned about the rejection, he was upset. He wanted it to be done the way he wanted it done and not how the court said it needed to happen. He was pissed off that they rejected the application and required them to complete a child support affidavit. Keisha agreed to exclude it from the original application at Tyler's demand. The court required a child support worksheet along with some other specifics, so they suggested that Tyler and Keisha proceed with counsel. Tyler found someone and told Keisha they would get it set back up to be processed. Keisha acknowledged it and moved on. During the process of waiting, Keisha decided to have a garage sale to clean out some of the stuff in the house they didn't need anymore.

Everything she planned to sell belonged to her and the kids and she wanted to use the money to cover a few things around the house since Tyler wasn't contributing financially. She planned out the garage sale and asked one of her friends to help her set it up and advertise it. Before Keisha could have the garage sale, the court responded to their second application and scheduled a hearing. They went to the hearing and learned more about the process of separation and divorce. They were still speaking to one another, and Tyler would still stop by the house. It seemed to be going smooth until one day when Tyler came over to see Keisha and he got upset with her because she didn't want to participate in his pity party.

Instead of calming down and leaving, Tyler pushed Keisha onto the floor and told her, "That's why you were raped! You're weak! Look at you! You got what you deserved! You probably liked it! Stupid whore!"

Keisha was in shock...she could not believe what was happening.

"Leave Tyler." is all she could find the strength to say as she pulled herself up off the floor.

Tyler kept taunting her until he was satisfied then he left. Keisha checked on her children and it seemed like they were oblivious to what happened. She got them all cleaned up and ready for bed. They said their prayers and she tucked them in for the night. Keisha went to her room, closed the door, and turned on the shower. She got in and slid down the wall until her body couldn't slide anymore. She just sat there mixing tears and water. She didn't know what to do from there. She felt so broken and destroyed. She felt isolated and dismissed. She didn't know who to talk to about what was going on or if she should even try to talk to anyone about it. She was afraid for herself and her children.

Keisha was an unemployed student who would soon have to add 'single mom' to her list of titles. It was draining all the life from her. She felt like Tyler was going to continue this type of behavior. She was unsure of what he would do next and felt like she always had to be on guard. It became nearly impossible to stay focused on course work. Keisha didn't want to take the kids out much because Tyler took the vehicle with working A/C and the leather seats in his car with no A/C was not a good mix in the middle of summer. She felt trapped in the house while waiting for Tyler to come back and react to something else.

A week went by and there was no Tyler. It was a stressful week because Keisha stayed on edge. She couldn't relax, sleep, or eat. She was miserable. Every day Keisha would continue to gather things for the garage sale and prepared for her and the kids to get their own place soon. When they went to the first divorce hearing, the judge ordered Tyler to start contributing to Keisha and the kids. Since they were still living in the marital house, she wasn't receiving a lot of financial assistance from Tyler because he paid the bills. Since Keisha was so uncomfortable in the house, she started looking for places to move as soon as the judge ordered Tyler to help. A second week passed with no visit from Tyler. Although Keisha was extremely grateful, she was growing more and more afraid with every week that passed without a visit.

As she was cleaning out her stuff, she was reminded of the good times. She smiled thinking about the fun they had. She was so happy when she reminisced on the good times in their marriage. Those moments made her feel like she did the right thing. Those moments made her feel like she didn't fail. She cried as each memory faded and she drifted back into reality. As she wiped away her tears, she thought to herself, 'It was fun while it lasted'. She slowly started to see that she had been alone in the marriage for quite some time. All the fond memories she thought about came with a plethora of tumultuous moments and a river of tears. The fun she was trying to hold on to was replaced by the truth...she was realizing how the good times and funny memories are nothing more than tainted truths. In that moment Keisha understood that she was just a pawn in Tyler's game of chess.

Another week passed without a visit from Tyler but at this point, Keisha was cool. She was used to how their life had been with no contact from Tyler. The kids didn't seem to even notice that Tyler had not been around. It was becoming the new normal and Keisha was starting to get comfortable with the peace. A few days later, Tyler called.

"Hey...how you doin'?" He asked.

"Hi. I'm good." Keisha responded.

"How the kids doing?" Tyler questioned.

"They are good. You can come see them whenever you want." She told him.

"Yeah. I'm probably gone come by there later. Is that ok?" He inquired.

"That's fine Tyler." Keisha said.

As they ended the call, Keisha thought it was strange that he asked for her permission to do anything because that was very unlike him. His behavior was a little off-putting for Keisha. In her experience, when Tyler was nice, it was simply the calm before the storm. Yet and still, she went with it and waited for Tyler to stop by. She tried to avoid leaving the house so she wouldn't miss him. By the time Keisha finished dinner, Tyler still had not arrived. She proceeded with her nightly ritual with the kids and then put them down for bed. Just before she was about to take her shower, she heard the garage door open. A few seconds later, she saw Tyler appear in the kitchen walkway.

"Hey," he said when he saw Keisha walking out of the bedroom.

"Hey Tyler." She responded with an attitude.

"Where the kids at? How they doin'?" Tyler asks looking around.

"They are asleep Tyler. It's after 9 o'clock. I thought you were gonna come over earlier, while they were still up." Keisha explained.

"I was, but something came up. I'm here now though!" He said.

"But the kids are asleep." She repeated.

Tyler walked towards her and said "I'll see them next time. I wanted to see you."

Keisha could not believe what she was hearing. "Tyler," she interrupted, "I'm not doing this with you."

"What you mean?" He asked seeming confused.

"You said you were coming to see the kids. You told me you were coming earlier to see them, but you get here after they are in bed." She explained.

"Ok Keisha. I'll come see them one day next week then. Is that what you want?" He replied.

"Whatever Tyler." Keisha sighed.

Shortly after, Tyler left. The following week, he did the same thing. He waited until the kids were in bed before he came to visit. Keisha was extremely annoyed by this because it was evident to her that he had no intentions on actually visiting the kids.

"Why don't you come by during the day when they are awake and running around? I know they would love to see you." Keisha asked.

"I'm trying Keisha but it's not that easy." He tried to explain.

"How is it not that easy Tyler? You choose when to visit and I am not impeding on your vision." She told him.

"It's just hard right now." He said with animosity in every word.

"They haven't seen you in weeks Tyler. They miss you. They want to see you." She attempted to explain.

"I'll talk to you later Keisha." Tyler said as he walked out the door.

Minutes later, Keisha heard the garage door open and close. She went in her room and cried. She couldn't believe that Tyler didn't want to see their kids. She could not understand why he was avoiding them. They were growing up and changing so fast. She couldn't imagine not being around them, which is why it was hard for her to understand how Tyler could go so long without being around them. Keisha realized then, in that moment, she was now a single parent. Since Tyler was already avoiding them, it seemed like this would be their new normal and she would be alone raising the kids. From what she was already experiencing, she also knew this was going to be very hard. Keisha knew things would be even harder for the kids. Nevertheless, she kept going through the motions to get them to their next checkpoint. The garage sale was a week away.

CHAPTER SEVEN

Let the Games Begin

On the day of the sale, Keisha and her friend set up and sold the items they had available. Once they were done, they cleaned up and Keisha's friend left. About an hour later, Tyler came over to the house. He walked in and demanded that Keisha give him half of her earnings from the garage sale. She refused but he insisted. He even made the claim that half of the money was his anyway since they are still married, and Keisha sold stuff he bought for her. She refused again and told him he wasn't entitled to anything. She explained to him that what she sold was not anything he purchased for her, and she all of the money she made was hers. He continued to argue and tell her that half of the money was his.

He asked how much she made, and Keisha told him a number smaller than what she actually earned. After arguing with Tyler for nearly 30 minutes, Keisha decided to give him half of what she told him she earned hoping that he would accept it and leave. Tyler took the money and continued to argue at Keisha. Keisha was so numb... she had no more energy left to argue. Shortly after, Tyler decided to leave.

Keisha showered and attempted to lay down but couldn't sleep. She kept hearing a voice loudly in her head. The voice was as clear as her children calling her name. She heard the voice telling her to go into the kitchen and grab the knife from the dish rack. She couldn't understand why she was hearing this voice or why it was instructing her to get a knife from the dish rack. She heard the voices get more stern with each demand and then it stopped when Keisha finally refused. She still didn't get why this voice wanted her to have a knife so badly.

She turned on some relaxing music and closed her eyes to go to sleep. She slept for about an hour before she was started out of her sleep by the garage door opening. She hopped up and threw on a house dress to see what was going on. Before she could reach the kitchen Tyler was coming through the garage door into the house with a mission.

"I want to talk to you about the divorce Keisha." Tyler demanded.

"I have nothing left to say Tyler." Keisha responded with a deflated tone.

"Either talk to me about the divorce or I'm about to start tearing shit up!" Tyler told Keisha.

Keisha just stood there and told Tyler, "I'm done talking."

"Ok then". Tyler said before he proceeded to destroy Keisha's sorority stuff by cutting it up and tearing it apart.

Keisha attempted to grab her purse from one of the bags and Tyler almost cut her arm. Keisha barely grabbed her purse from the bag just before Tyler made the final cut to it. She stood by the bed and waited for him to finish. When he stopped, he had destroyed all her sorority items in his sight that were in the bedroom.

He looked at Keisha and asked, "You ready to talk now?"

Keisha simply responded and said, "No."

Tyler walked out of the room for a few seconds and returned with a surprise for Keisha. He looked at her and told her, "I probably bought this too" right before he doused her with bleach.

Moments later, Keisha grabbed her dog and took it over to the area where her kids were sleeping before she walked out the front door. Keisha looked to her right and to her left before she began walking to the neighbor's home. She got to the front door and rang the bell asking for help from her neighbor. When her neighbor answered the door, she took one look at Keisha and told her to come inside. She closed the door behind Keisha, but she quickly opened it back up because of the smell.

"Is that you?" Her neighbor asked.

"Yes. I'm sorry. I need help. My husband just threw bleach on me. I need to call the police because my kids are still in the house." Keisha explained.

Her neighbor quickly found her cell phone and placed the call for Keisha. "Yes, my neighbor is standing in my house covered in bleach! Her husband poured it on her and her kids are still in the house." She told dispatch.

Keisha's neighbor gave the information to the cops regarding the address and description of Tyler. She ended the call and turned to Keisha.

"What happened?" Her neighbor asked.

Keisha told her the details and begin to cry. Her neighbor consoled her and revealed that she had a similar experience with her children's father. They swapped stories while they waited on the police to arrive. Less than 10 minutes later, Keisha and her neighbor saw red and blue lights flashing through the windows. The officer was instructed not to knock on the neighbor's door to prevent Tyler from knowing where Keisha was. The officers arrived at Keisha and Tyler's front door and was greeted by a sweat drenched Tyler.

They told him they received a call and asked to enter. He allowed them to go inside without hesitation. Once they passed the threshold, the smell of bleach overpowered them, and they had to exit to regroup. Once they gathered themselves, they went back into the home to see what had been done. After they walked through, they came to the neighbor's house. When Keisha came out, she saw Tyler in the back of the cop car. She was not prepared to see the damage Tyler had done in the home...especially, in the master bedroom area. The first thing she did was check on her children to make sure they weren't hurt in any way. She found them unharmed and still asleep. She saw the damage Tyler did and all she could do was wait for the next steps. A few days later, Tyler was released from police custody after his cousin bailed him out. A little over a week later, Keisha had to go to court for a domestic violence hearing to expedite a restraining order.

During the hearing Keisha was offered the house, the truck, and financial assistance. Keisha declined taking the house due to everything that was going on. She agreed to be out of the house within the next couple of months. Tyler and Keisha didn't speak much at this point. They only communicated through the court system. It all escalated to a point of no return. A few weeks later, Keisha and the kids moved into their new place. Due to the way everything popped off, Tyler was not allowed to know any information about where Keisha and the kids were living. Keisha started to feel more secure after they left the house. For some reason, Keisha felt more secure being away from the house but often had an eerie feeling every time she left home. She always felt like someone was watching her. Nevertheless, Keisha kept moving forward, creating a better life for her and the kids as she was still in school. After about a month, Keisha started to move about with a little less hesitation.

One day, Keisha and the kids returned from a night at church and got into their apartment as usual. She got the kids ready for bed and started working on her course assignments. She was so tired that she fell asleep while studying. Moments after she fell asleep, she was startled awake by her neighbor beating on her apartment door.

"Hey! Hey! Wake Up!" Keisha faintly heard in her sleep. There was a pause followed by more banging on the door.

"Hey! Are you in there? Come out here! Please open the door!" Keisha finally woke up and answered the door.

She wiped her eyes and responded, "Hey, what's going on?"

Her neighbor moved back and invited her to step out the door.

When Keisha stepped out, she saw a bright light just before she heard her neighbor ask, "Is that your truck?" Keisha walked out to the edge of the balcony and saw her truck engulfed in flames.

"Yes. That's my truck. It must mean that God has something better in store for me." Keisha said calmly when she saw the truck.

Her neighbor was hysterical! She told Keisha the fire department had already been called. Keisha thanked her neighbor and went back into her apartment. Later that morning, Keisha contacted her lawyer and told her what happened. A couple days later, she found out that Tyler was indicted on felony charges for what happened the night he doused her with bleach. He was charged with one count of simple battery, one count of simple assault, and destruction of property. He was charged a couple of days before the truck was set on fire. After he was charged, he posted a picture of him and Keisha on fire with the caption 'Death to Dishonor' on his social media pages. With all this information, Keisha's lawyer knew Tyler would be facing additional charges. To their surprise, Tyler was cleared of the truck fire due to a lack of evidence.

Just like that, Keisha was left without transportation for her and the kids. She had to speak with the fire department, the insurance company, the apartment complex, the police department, and lawyers to prove that she was not the one who started the fire. She couldn't believe that this was happening. She was quickly moved from the victim to the suspect. One of the hardest things Keisha had to do during this time was explain to the children why their truck was sitting outside the apartment burnt. There was so much she couldn't answer. She hated that she even had to worry about this. She was confused by a lot of it herself. Keisha did what she knew best and that was to keep going through the motions. She had to keep it together for the kids. She wanted to keep their lives as normal as possible.

Despite her best efforts, Keisha had to make some major adjustments quickly. After the courts caught wind of what happened to Keisha's truck, they ordered Tyler to give up his car to Keisha and the kids. Keisha called a few of her friends to accompany her to the police station to pick up the car. Keisha's friends knew Tyler and even gave him a ride back home after Keisha drove off with the car. After they dropped Tyler off, they went to Keisha's apartment to talk to her about what happened. When they got there, they immediately told Keisha everything Tyler said. Tyler told Keisha's friend that she was keeping the kids away from him. He told them that he would just wait until the kids are old enough to make their own decisions and try to see them then.

Tyler also said that Keisha was being irrational and unreasonable. He didn't feel like he did anything wrong. All of this was happening in the middle of waiting for a hearing date to finalize the divorce. Keisha was ready for all of this to be over so that she could move forward in her life. She felt like this was keeping her in a chaotic state of being and she despised it. She wanted to be free of Tyler's grip. Keisha's friends stayed with her for a few hours before heading back home. The next day Keisha's lawyer called.

"Hi Keisha. How are you?" Just asked.

"I'm well Judy. How are you?" Keisha responded.

"I'm great Keisha, Thanks. I'm calling because we finally have a date for the hearing." Judy explained.

"Judy, that is good news. What's the date?" Keisha inquired.

"December 3rd is your hearing date. At the hearing, we should be completing the divorce proceedings and getting the judge to sign off on everything." Judy told Keisha.

They spent several minutes discussing what the hearing should look like, what Keisha would need to do, and what should happen next. Since the hearing was still a few weeks out, Keisha did what her lawyer told her to do in preparation and continued to work on her school assignments. A few days before the hearing she learned some disturbing news. This was not the time for Keisha to be derailed by bad news. Regardless of what Keisha wanted to happen, she had to deal with what the reality of what was actually happening.

"I'm sorry Keisha, I know this is not what you wanted to hear." Judy said to Keisha after breaking the news to her.

"I don't understand...how this could be happening?!" Keisha responded with confusion.

"Well Keisha, since Tyler decided to get a lawyer less than a week before the hearing, the judge will not proceed unless he allows Tyler's lawyer enough time to go over the case and learn how to best assist Tyler." Judy explained. "Due to the limited time between hiring his lawyer and the hearing, the court date must be rescheduled." Judy continued.

Keisha listened with tears in her eyes and rage bubbling up from the soles of her feet. She was crushed. She felt like Tyler was still controlling her life and what she was doing. It was like he had delayed hiring a lawyer on purpose in order to cause a stir. It seemed as if someone was helping him plan these distractions. Whatever it was, Keisha couldn't understand how things seemed to keep working in favor of Tyler.

"So, we have to wait all the way until April for that?" Keisha asked.

"Unfortunately, we do. That is the next available date on the judge's docket." Judy explained.

Keisha and Judy spoke about the change to the hearing date and the details about the divorce moving forward. Judy attempted to comfort Keisha as best she could, but Keisha was obviously starting to break. Keisha realized that things would continue to be a struggle as long as Tyler had control over anything. As a result, Keisha started working to help eliminate Tyler's control.

Keisha was ready for this to be over so when April came, she showed up to the hearing eager to close out the marriage. She was glad that Tyler didn't pull any more stunts before the hearing. However, she learned shortly after the start of their hearing that Tyler had plenty more tricks up his sleeve and he was very strategic with his next moves.

When the judge mentioned custody, Tyler declined to discuss it and told the judge, "She can have them."

Due to the incident after the garage sale, Tyler was only offered supervised visitation with the children. He was so upset by that offer that he cussed Judy out. This was his opportunity to discuss everything and get the resolve he expressed that he wanted. Keisha thought his reaction to the judge was strange since he was so enraged by the thought of supervised visitation.

When the judge heard Tyler's response, he questioned him, "Excuse me? So, you do NOT want to discuss the custody of your children?"

Tyler told the judge the same thing he told him before,

"She can have them. I'll pay whatever I need to pay but she can have them."

The judge was appalled by Tyler's response and as a result, placed a permanent restraining order against Tyler since he expressed that he didn't want anything to do with their children. Tyler shrugged his shoulders and the proceedings continued. The judge attempted to set up child support requirements and learned that Tyler was now unemployed and out of the military and could no longer afford the amount he was paying while he was working. The judge required Keisha to keep insurance for the children and cover the costs of anything they wanted to do regarding camps, daycare, etc. since she was now working. At the same time, Tyler's child support payments decreased by more than half. Keisha was pissed! She felt like Tyler getting his way again and the children were being dismissed but there was nothing she could do.

A month later, the final divorce decree arrived in the mail. Keisha looked at it and thought that things were finally over. A few days later, a woman came into Keisha's job looking to buy something for her husband. The person who helped her was Keisha's friend, Layla. Layla worked in the cubicle next to Keisha so Keisha could hear the entire conversation between Layla and the customer. As Layla is gathering the customer's information, Keisha recognized a lot of her responses. The customer gave Keisha's last name and former address as her own. When Keisha heard this, she felt her blood stop flowing and pure rage filled her veins. All the information revealed to Keisha that this customer was Tyler's new wife!

Keisha walked past Layla's cubicle to catch a glimpse of this lady who took her place. When she walked behind her, she saw the customer had a 6-month-old baby with her. Keisha walked to the front of the store and told her manager what was happening. Shortly after, Layla walked up to the front and revealed the severity of a possible situation. Layla told the management team to keep Keisha in the back until the customer left. Keisha was stunned by what she had just found out. Tyler was building a whole new family while he was destroying theirs!

CHAPTER EIGHT

Transfer

It was a whole new world for Keisha. It was a whole new life for Tyler. It seemed so surreal...as if it was all a bad dream that Keisha wished she could wake up from. After everything calmed down at work, Keisha started to focus on keeping up with her success. She was doing very well at work and still doing fairly well in class. She felt like she could bounce back from this latest drama and come out better than before. Although Keisha was progressing at work and in school, she was not progressing emotionally and mentally. It was like she was always being watched. Her classes quickly started to become too much for her to handle as she switched gears to focus on her mental and emotional health.

She could no longer commit to the demands of school and work full time with no support. She was taking on more responsibility at work and slowly, school was put on the back burner. There was no possible way for Keisha to do it all alone. She was struggling trying to work and keep the kids in extracurricular activities. She wanted to keep their lives as 'normal' as possible. She wanted to work, finish school, and move into her career, but the effects of the divorce were taking a toll on her and she realized she couldn't manager everything on her own. Keisha did all she could in her courses before she completely stopped. While on her break from school, she thought she would have more time to focus on her well-being, but that was not the case.

It was a hard choice to make because it was a setback in Keisha's plan, but it was the only option. Being out of school haunted Keisha. She felt like she failed herself because she had to take a break. She also felt like she couldn't leave her kids with anyone because she didn't know if Tyler would be able to get to them. Since the fire, Keisha never really felt safe. She always felt like someone was always watching her...like she couldn't move without looking over her shoulder. She talked to her manager about how she was feeling, and her manager told her that the company was expanding and there was a possible position for her in a new location. She told them she was interested, and about a month later, Keisha and her kids were moving nearly 2 hours away to a new place. She was so happy to have the opportunity to relocate and regain some peace!

Keisha and the kids moved into their new home and Keisha was given a couple days off to get settled. They were in a whole new area with little to no support, but it felt safer than being where they were. When Keisha arrived at work, she was informed that she would have a new position. Not only was she relocated, but she was also now in management! She received a raise in her new position! She was so excited! The first few days of work were so full of excitement. Keisha was meeting new people and learning about her new neighborhood. By Wednesday of the first week, Keisha learned that there were some challenges with this new location and new position.

"Keisha you'll be working on Saturday to make sure we have an internet manager on duty." Her manager told her.

"My daycare is closed on Saturday. I don't have anyone to watch my kids for me." Keisha responded.

"It won't be a problem to bring them with you. Your office is pretty big. Just keep them in there and make sure they aren't running around." He told Keisha.

At this point her only response was, "Ok."

After a few weeks of this, Keisha asked why the internet manager, who didn't have kids, couldn't work on Saturdays. She was never given a valid reason. This did not sit well with Keisha. Shortly after she inquired about the scheduling, she learned that she was the only manager who was paid hourly. This infuriated Keisha! She felt like she was being taken advantage of because of her situation. It made no sense to have two people with the same title with one of them being treated like a manager while the other was treated like an average worker.

Keisha was doing more in this position but was being treated like she was incompetent. She couldn't understand why she could not catch a break. When Keisha learned she was being excluded from management meetings, she had had enough! She was not going to be the 'nice girl' anymore. She confronted the rest of the management team again. During this confrontation, it was made clear that people of color where not meant to advance when there was a white person being considered or already in a similar position. Keisha could not believe what she was experiencing! At the end of the week Keisha put in her notice that she would not be returning to work due to the way the company operated. She quickly had to find a new place of employment.

Keisha bounced around for a few months looking for a job that was a good fit for her. She eventually found a temporary job that seemed to be full of promise. It was a state job through an agency but there was an opportunity to become permanent within six months. Before she even reached the six- month mark, Keisha was offered a full-time position. She was overjoyed! She was finally in a position where she felt like she could advance. For Keisha and the kids, it seemed like things were looking up. Keisha was a quick learner and soon exceeded her superiors' expectations. The more Keisha showed her value, the more responsibility she was given. It was nice. Keisha felt like she was appreciated in her position by her supervisor. It was a nice change.

Although things were looking up for Keisha at work, she was still struggling with being alone. It was not how she saw her life progressing. Yet and still, she had to move forward and adjust. There was little time to spend thinking about the life she thought she would have at this moment. The kids were growing up fast and Keisha was barely staying afloat. She was used to handling things on her own and that's just what she did. Day by day, Keisha fought hard to smile through the struggle. She was used to going through the motions and keeping her tribulations bottled up inside.

She didn't want to burden others with her problems. Keisha felt like this was her struggle to deal with and she had to do it with a forced smile and a tight lip. Sometimes she felt dumb or stupid about what she allowed to happen or for what she accepted. Sometimes she felt like she deserved the treatment because she chose Tyler. In her eyes, at times, this was her punishment. Regardless of what she felt and what she didn't do, she knew she couldn't give up. Keisha knew her kids were watching and depending on her success. One thing she wanted to teach her kids was to not settle for less than what they were worth. When she found out her salary was actually below the poverty line, she spoke up to her supervisor and requested an increase. He told her he would help her with this and would talk to his boss to get it all squared away. A couple of weeks went by and there was no communication with Keisha about fixing her salary. She went back to her supervisor, and they spoke to his boss together...however, the conversation did not go very well for Keisha. The manager offered to raise her salary if she would take on more responsibilities. Keisha felt like this was not fair treatment and declined the offer.

The manager was not a nice person and was already dealing with issues regarding discrimination with some other employees in the unit. Keisha knew this wouldn't last much longer. A part of her felt defeated but a part of her felt motivated. She understood she had to use what she had to get what she wanted. So, she started to work on creating the life she wanted for her and her kids. Many days, while sitting at her desk, Keisha started working on writing her first book. It seemed like a fair trade to Keisha. If she was going to do any extra work, it would be her own.

She used her downtime at work on compiling material for her book. She used the printers to print samples and included her coworkers by soliciting their opinions along the way. It didn't take long for her to have what she needed. Keisha had been writing since she was young, so she had plenty of material to pull from for her first book. She didn't know everything about publishing a book, but she knew enough to get it done. After nearly four weeks, Keisha had her first book completed. Her coworkers were so encouraging and supportive. She finally felt like she was on the right track!

Although Keisha was proud of her progress thus far, she knew she wasn't out of the woods just yet. Keisha occupied her mind with her book, but her reality was slowly creeping back in to slap her right in the face. A couple days after Keisha submitted her book to be reviewed, her lawyer reached out.

"Hey Keisha, how are you?" Judy said.

"I'm ok Judy, how are you?" Keisha responded unsure of what Judy was calling for.

"I'm good thanks. I'm calling to see if Tyler has given you any child support since court?" Judy asked.

"Well, he did in the beginning of the case, but I haven't received anything in the last two months." Keisha explained.

"Well, that means we have to file a contempt order and go back to court. I'll send you the date as soon as the clerk gets it to me." Judy said.

"Ok. Thanks Judy." Keisha said before ending the call.

It seemed like every other month after the first contempt date, Judy was calling to check and see if Keisha was still getting child support. Even though Tyler told the judge he would pay whatever, he wasn't keeping his end of the agreement. His only obligation was to pay what was ordered. When Tyler got the hearing postponed from December to April, it gave him the opportunity to complete his time with the military. When the April court date came, Tyler told the judge he was longer employed. As a result, the child support obligation was cut in half for Tyler.

What was strange to Keisha was the fact that he was having an issue paying, but the amount was greatly reduced, and this was all he had to do. At this point, Keisha knew Tyler was still playing games and this was another attempt to hurt her. Keisha was faced with dealing with this all on her own. Her military friends were gone. She was far away from any type of support. For so many reasons, she felt hopeless. She felt like this cycle would never be over as long as Tyler controlled a part of her life. At this point, he was affecting her ability to financially support HIS children. In her mind, it seemed like Tyler felt like he had something to prove. She just didn't know who he was trying to prove it to.

About a week later, things started to look up. Keisha's cousin asked if she could stay with Keisha while she got on her feet. Keisha happily welcomed her with open arms. Keisha was so happy to have someone there with her. Even if it was temporary, she was grateful for the help and the company. Her cousin saw firsthand what she was dealing with, but she admired Keisha's hustle and drive. However, after a few months, her cousin grew tired of staying with Keisha...she wanted to get out in the new area and do her own thing. Their relationship started to struggle as a result. That's when it happened...

"Keisha?" The voice on the other end of the phone said softly with an emotional tone. "You need to go see Dad." The voice continued.

It was one of Keisha's brothers. He told her that their dad Gerald was in hospice and was holding on waiting to see her. Keisha immediately informed her job about the situation, then asked her cousin to keep an eye on the girls while she and her son went to see her father. When Keisha and her son arrived at the hospital, they were greeted by a few of her other siblings. Her sister took her and her son up to the room to see Gerald. Her sister told Keisha she would let her have some alone time with Gerald and she took Keisha's son with her. Keisha decided to stay the night in Gerald's hospice room on the pull-out couch.

She read the DNR information next to his bed and saw the bracelet on his arm. Keisha's heart sank. She knew that Gerald was done fighting and that this was the end. Gerald survived 10 strokes, a heart condition, hypertension, glaucoma and was diabetic. He had been suffering for a few months after the last round of strokes, unbeknownst to Keisha. She spent her time with her father telling him that she would be ok and that she loved him. As Keisha hugged Gerald and assured him that she was ok with him letting go, she saw tears fall from his eyes. Those last moments she spent with him were priceless for both of them.

Keisha finally laid down to get some rest after she spent time loving on her father. In the middle of the night, she heard his breathing change. The sound of each breath grew louder and louder. Keisha jumped up and called the nurse. It was a terrifying moment for Keisha. The nurse was able to give Gerald more pain medicine to keep him comfortable and they went back to sleep. The next morning, she met her sister in the lobby with her son and drove back home. Three days later, one of Keisha's brothers called, "Keisha, he's gone."

CHAPTER NINE

The Struggle Gets Real

Keisha felt so emotionally drained. It was extremely difficult for her to see her father laid to rest. When she returned home, it was hard to adjust to not having her father. She spoke with her cousin and asked her to start looking for places to move because things seemed to be getting more and more complicated between them. Her cousin understood and began looking right away. After a few weeks of looking, she found her own place and moved out. Once her cousin left, Keisha was alone...again. She appreciated her cousin staying and helping but she was glad to have the house to herself again. She felt like this was the first step to getting back to herself. However, when Keisha returned to work, she learned she still had a long journey ahead of her.

More frequently, she was tested by the manager at her job. Keisha had no problem speaking her mind. They would bump heads most times because he would say something off the wall and expect Keisha to just accept whatever he said without question. That was not the way Keisha operated. The constant court dates and random child support payments made it more of a struggle for Keisha to stay consistent with bills and daycare. Keisha completed her book right before her dad passed. When she started researching how much it would cost to print the books, Keisha put the project on hold. Everything seemed to be going against Keisha and she didn't know what to do. Just when Keisha thought it couldn't get any worse, she found out more devastating news.

"Hello, may I speak to Keisha please?" the voice asked.

"This is Keisha. How may I help you?" she responded.

"I'm calling from the victim's advocacy office. This is a courtesy call to notify you that all charges against Tyler have been dropped." the voice told Keisha.

She didn't know how to respond or why this was happening. She asked a few questions but there were very few answers. The most they told her was that 'due to HIPAA regulations they could not disclose more information.' She was oblivious to what was going on. She just knew she didn't like it. The last thing Keisha heard about Tyler's case was that he was charged. The victim's advocate contacted Keisha again and asked to meet with her in the office at once. During that meeting, Keisha was told that her testimony would be needed, and Tyler was facing felony charges.

She informed Keisha of her limited available resources and said they would be in touch. Many months had passed between the last time Keisha heard from them and now. She was under the impression that they would reach out again, before this moment, with different news. She was expecting to go to court, but this news was bittersweet. She was relieved about not having to appear in court, but she was also upset that the charges were dropped. Keisha felt like Tyler would not be held responsible for his actions. She thought he would have to explain to a judge why he did what he did. She thought he would have to justify why he felt it was ok to disrespect Keisha the way he did. She felt like he should explain his carelessness when he destroyed so much inside the house. She wanted him to explain what drove him to cut up her clothes, shoes, purses, and stuff.

Keisha could not wrap her mind around the fact that Tyler threw bleach on her, destroyed the house, and was able to just walk away. It seemed like she was being punished for something that was done to her. This was unreal! She couldn't believe this. 'Why was he getting off so easy after all of this?' Keisha kept thinking to herself. That phone call from the victim's advocate changed everything. In the midst of the news, Keisha had to make some quick life changing decisions. She was finally starting to believe in herself and her talent as a writer. She was starting to think she could actually be successful with this writing stuff. With everything going the way it was, Keisha was also a little afraid of how she was going to make things happen.

She didn't have the answers, but she knew that something would pan out for her. With the lack of consistent financial support from Tyler, Keisha struggled to live her dream and maintain her family. Before she knew it, Keisha was faced with the choice to pay rent or print the first set of books. She felt like printing the books would be a great investment in herself. She also knew that rent still needed to be paid so books had to be sold. Keisha didn't talk to anyone about her dilemma. As usual, Keisha did what she felt was best for her and the kids. In this moment, she felt like getting her books sold was worth the risk.

In her mind, investing in her books and her writing was

important. She had come so far and accomplished so much, she just wanted to continue to grow and not be stuck anymore. A couple days later she contacted the printer and placed her order. Within days Keisha held copies of her first book. It was such an amazing feeling! She felt so proud! She shared the news with everyone she knew and before she knew it, she was selling copies left and right. Keisha felt so accomplished. She was able to work something out with her complex regarding her rent so that she didn't risk eviction. She was officially an author!

It was an amazing feeling for her. There was nothing that could ruin this moment for Keisha. She was overjoyed. Keisha started to promote her book to her coworkers and to others on social media. Book sales were going well for Keisha. She reached out to her cousin living in the area to help promote the book at local malls.

"Is there anything specific you want me to say to people about the book?" her cousin asked.

Keisha explained what she wanted her to do, and they set out to gain new customers. Keisha's cousin introduced her to someone who could relate to her story. In that moment, Keisha knew she couldn't quit. Within the first two weeks of selling her books, she sold enough copies to cover her rent. As her excitement grew about being an author, she remembered something else she wanted to do...complete school. Keisha didn't like to leave things incomplete. What she started, she liked to finish, even if it took her a while to do so. Keisha started thinking about how she would incorporate school back into her schedule.

She started looking at her transcript, talking to advisors

and gathering as much information as possible. She wanted to make sure she would be able to complete the program without any interruptions. The more information she received about her program, she realized she wouldn't be able to complete this program without the support of her village. After multiple phone calls and discovery conversations, Keisha and her advisor reached an 'ah ha' moment.

"Well Keisha, you could use the courses you've already completed towards a different program that will allow you to work closely to the field you wanted to initially work in. The only difference is you'll have to take a few more courses instead of completing a practicum. In addition to that, this program will not allow you to be on track to become licensed when you complete the degree. You would have to check with your state to find out what their requirements are for licensure with your degree." the advisor told Keisha.

She was happy that she could complete her degree in roughly a year, but she was a little disappointed that she had to change programs. At this point, Keisha was just looking forward to moving forward. She had already been through so much. She was ready for a fresh start.

CHAPTER TEN

Try it Again

At this point so much was changing and shifting in Keisha's life. It seemed as if she was on a wild roller coaster ride that would not end. One moment things were great and in the next, just horrible. After a while, Keisha felt like things were becoming more stable and she wanted to do whatever she needed to do in order to keep it that way. As a result, Keisha decided to take a critical look at her struggles and figure out how to handle any future obstacles so she could continue to progress. One of the main things Keisha needed was support. She was so far away from everyone she knew and loved... the people who could help her. She looked at her finances and realized just how unstable they were. She looked at her job and the way she was being treated. She looked at her living arrangements and she decided she needed to change a lot of things in her life.

She felt like moving back to the area she was familiar with would be good for book sales, support, and financial stability. The area was much more affordable, and Keisha knew what to do. She contacted her old boss and asked for her old job back. Then she put in her two weeks' notice at the current job.

As soon as it was worked out with the jobs, Keisha started looking for places to live. This was extremely difficult because Keisha didn't have any savings and needed a hefty amount to relocate.

"I saw on social media that you're moving, are you going back home?" Keisha's friend Krissy messaged her.

"No. I'm moving back there!" Keisha responded.

"Oh wow, ok! Do you already have a place to live?" Krissy asked.

"No, not yet." Keisha wrote back.

"Y'all can stay with me and Ian if you want. Your son can share the room with Ian, the girls can have their own room and you can have the couch. Is that cool?" Krissy offered.

Keisha was blown away by Krissy's offer. "Thank you so much! It won't be for that long, I promise. Thank you, Krissy!!!" Keisha wrote back full of excitement.

She felt like everything was falling into place. She looked at how it was all working out and saw it was necessary to take a few steps back so that she could move forward again. Keisha and the kids arrived at Krissy's house and started to get settled in. It was like a refreshing reunion. Although Krissy and Keisha kept in touch while Keisha was away, Keisha didn't feel so alone anymore. The kids were happy to be around people they knew before they left. Everything was going the way it needed to and it felt good. Keisha's job was scheduled to start the week after her and the kids moved back.

This gave her enough time to get the kids situated in school and to get setup for the next month at Krissy's. When Keisha went back to work, one of the questions she was asked most was about Tyler and his new wife. Most of the people who were there during the previous incident were still working there when Keisha returned. The silliest and most annoying question she was asked was "What kind of stuff you got to make a man act like that?" Each time they asked her, Keisha attempted to laugh it off as if it didn't bother her. However, she was starting to believe that it was something she did to cause Tyler to flip out like that.

Everyone in the city knew about Keisha's case although it was never publicized. The nature of the situation was so unique that it circulated heavily amongst the local fire and police departments. It didn't take long for Keisha to realize she was being recognized for all the wrong reasons. After a few weeks, Keisha found a place for her and the kids to move into. She told Krissy the good news, but she was not super excited. She enjoyed having Keisha and the kids there with her and Ian, but at the same time, she understood. The move-in date was about 10 days away. Keisha and the kids begin to pack and prepare to move into their new place. When they arrived, it felt like a weight was lifted and they were regaining themselves. All the excitement quickly wore off and reality slapped Keisha in the face again.

"Hey Keisha, how are you, It's Judy?" Keisha heard from the other end of the phone.

"Hey Judy, I'm fine. Is everything ok?" she asked.

"Well, I received your message about you moving back. Just wanted to be clear, you do know that Tyler is still living here in town at the same address?" Judy inquired.

Keisha couldn't believe this. She didn't consider this being an issue. When she looked further into it, she learned that she was within walking distance from Tyler and his new family. Since Tyler was still so close, Keisha had to update all the children's school information to include a copy of the restraining order, a photo description of Tyler, and a copy of the divorce decree proving Keisha had sole custody. She went from feeling refreshed to feeling overwhelmed.

As a result, she kept her children very close to her and refrained from going a lot of places. She didn't publicly update her location and only people she trusted knew where she was. Most of the people who knew were the people she worked with. Since Keisha was back at the same location she was at when Tyler's wife showed up, she had to provide them with a copy of the restraining order and photos of Tyler so they could help keep Keisha safe. Keisha felt like a spectacle. She felt like everyone was looking at her differently.

Keisha felt like she and her children were pitied by onlookers. It was weird. All of a sudden, everyone was treating her like she was fragile. The fear of running into Tyler made Keisha very anxious. She was extremely concerned about her children seeing him while they were on a school field trip or other outing. When Keisha got the news from Judy, the roller coaster of life threw in some new turns and flips to the non-stop ride. Keisha was all over the place mentally. She felt like every break came with crazy ass obstacles to overcome and she didn't know how much more she could take. Keisha needed to focus on the positive things that were happening for them. She was still selling her books and her coworkers were very supportive.

One coworker in particular, Lee, went out of his way to help Keisha with whatever she needed. Lee's support was like a blanket on a cold night to Keisha. She was so grateful to have him in her corner. Anytime Keisha had an idea on how to increase book sales, Lee was down to help. He would walk the lot and solicit sales from customers, coworkers, and management. Keisha did not like to be the face of her product, so she was very happy that Lee was more than willing to step in on her behalf. Although Keisha and Lee were close before she moved, their friendship grew even stronger when she returned. Lee and a few other coworkers made the transition back to town a little easier to manage. There was so much Keisha had to readjust to…her living situation being the first. Although her new place wasn't the best, it was a fresh start. The rent wasn't too high, and the bills weren't expensive either. The neighborhood was not exactly where Keisha wanted to be with her children, but it was what she had to do for now to get to where she needed to be. By living there, she was in a better position to get on her feet completely without needing assistance. She wanted to be completely independent. She was tired of struggling but she would not quit.

It was hard for Keisha to move back to a place that is a source of so much pain and suffering for her. She moved away to obtain peace and to escape. She thought she would be able to replace those feelings and memories by just leaving them there and walking away. She went through so much and told no one. She was still very broken. She spoke to one of her friends and they suggested that Keisha she go to therapy. She knew how beneficial it would be but she was leery due to a few bad experiences with therapists in the past. She had to learn to assess each situation based on itself, not on another situations. This was the key to Keisha learning how to cope and move forward, so she found another therapist and began her healing journey.

After the first session Keisha felt safe and supported by her therapist and looked forward to continuing the process. She knew it would require her to relive a lot of trauma, pain, and horrible moments but she also knew the benefits that would follow. Since Keisha was labeled as a domestic violence victim, she received her therapy sessions at no cost. She was glad she didn't have to pay but she despised being labeled a victim. During therapy, Keisha learned a lot about herself and her previous decision-making process. She learned how her past experiences influenced her current life. She was grateful for the journey of self-discovery and reflection. She didn't realize how far she had come until she got a call from Judy with more news. This time, Keisha felt better prepared to handle it.

"Hey Keisha." Judy said.

"Hi Judy." Keisha answered.

"So, my records show that you haven't received any child support payments in some time. Has Tyler sent you any payments directly that did not go through child support enforcement?" Judy asked.

"No, he hasn't sent anything to me. The child support portal shows that he is almost $10,000 in arrears." Keisha answered.

Judy confirmed that amount and they spoke about gathering all the documents and records to prepare to go back to court since ten grand in arrears is a felony. Keisha hated going to these contempt hearings though. They were always focused on Tyler in Keisha's opinion. She felt like they were working on his side to make things more convenient for him. He already didn't have any responsibility for them. He didn't have to take them to any doctor's appointments, help with any homework, or sit up with them when they weren't feeling well. He was able to wash his hands and live life free of the humans he helped create. All the emotions were hitting Keisha differently because Tyler was physically just five minutes away but he was so far gone in reality.

Since Keisha was concerned about the kids running into him while she was away from them, she started talking to them about what to do if they saw him. By this time, they were seven, eight and nine years old. Although Heaven was the oldest, she was the one who needed the most reminders about what to do. The younger two seemed to catch on fairly quick, but then they had questions. They wanted to know why their mom was telling them not to hug their dad if they saw him in public. They wanted to know why they couldn't talk to him if he called them by their name. They wanted to know why their dad was not allowed to be around them. They were curious children who wanted answers no matter how much they trusted their mom. Keisha attempted to explain everything to them the best way she could to help them understand.

"Well babies, your dad made some poor choices and those choices made him have to see a judge. The judge told your dad he couldn't be around you guys anymore. If he does, the judge will have him sent to jail and that is not what we want to happen. So, the best thing to do is follow the judge's order and not see or talk to your dad. When you turn 18, the judge will listen to you and may change his mind." Keisha explained.

"So, when I'm 18, the judge can't stop me from seeing daddy anymore?" Her son asked.

"Well, he will listen to you if you say you want to see your dad and he may change his mind and let dad see you." Keisha answered.

"But mommy, I'm only eight...that's 10 years away. I have to wait 10 years to be able to see daddy?" he asked.

"Yes baby. I'm sorry." Keisha said as she attempted to console her son.

His tears started to fall before she could even wrap her arms completely around him. It was one of the most difficult moments through the whole ordeal. Keisha felt like she failed her children by picking such a horrible father for them. She blamed herself for every bad feeling and situation they had experienced. She knew this was only the beginning of the questions. She anticipated more tears and disappointments. She realized the struggle was just getting ready to intensify. Keisha knew she had to shift her situation and change the direction of life for her children.

CHAPTER ELEVEN

New Beginning

It was hard for Keisha to wrap her mind around everything that was going on. It was literally like starting over. She had to retrain her brain. She had to learn how to live as a single mom and entrepreneur. She had to adjust to being "everything" for her children and for herself. She had to forget everything she learned that wasn't helping her grow. She had to adjust the way she was living to accommodate for the way she wanted to live. Keisha knew it would be a wild ride, but she was ready. The journey thus far was already something like a bad movie, so she was looking forward to the new beginning. One of the most exciting things about moving forward was becoming a full-time writer. She didn't want to work for anyone else any longer than she had to. The response she received after she released her first book was incredible!

It led her to believe that she could have a career as a writer. She wanted to continue to help others with her words. Keisha created a plan to accomplish that goal. She made a promise to herself that the upcoming year would be the last year she would work for someone else. Keisha had been self-employed many times in the past and loved the idea of working for herself. She loved the freedom of being able to move how she wanted to. She enjoyed having more control of her time.

Her plan was to invest in her business for an entire year so that she could become a full-time entrepreneur by the end of the year.

Keisha was successful in keeping her goals in check for the first few months of creating her plan. She stuck to her schedule after work and devoted a lot of time to making her dream come true. She was not the best at time management at the beginning of the process, but she worked hard to improve that skill. She learned to multi-task on a whole new level. She learned how to split her time between her kids, her dreams, her job, and her personal time. It was a challenging learning process, but Keisha was committed to making this work.

She was also invested in doing well at work. When she came back to work at her old job, she had her sights set on moving back up through the ranks as quickly as she could. She came back doing the same job she was doing before she moved away so it was like second nature to her at this point. When her manager put a competition in place for Keisha and her coworkers, she was super excited to show why she was so valuable. The competition lasted for a week and at the end of the week, the numbers were tallied, and the winner was announced. The prize included a weekend off from work, a hotel gift card, and a $100 cash prize as well. Just as Keisha expected, she won! Keisha was so proud of her accomplishment! Her performance made it easy to see why she was in the running for a promotion.

Two weeks later, Keisha celebrated her birthday and cashed in her prizes from the competition. When she returned to work, she was greeted with an extensive number of changes. She was told that these changes were made because of how things had gone while she was away. Most of the changes were more like small punishments instead of productivity improvements. Keisha told her manager that it was unfair for her to be penalized for the actions of her coworkers when she was not even there. Her manager challenged her logic and still wanted to hold her just as accountable as those who had been there. She refused to accept such nonsense and took the conversation up the chain of command to the general manager.

Keisha was so upset by the way things were being handled. Her general manager dismissed her concerns and instructed Keisha to settle it with her direct manager. Since they were not seeing eye to eye, the conversation didn't get them any closer to a resolution. After a few minutes of attempting to justify the decision once again with no luck, Keisha's manager told her to go home and come back in when she is ready to discuss the issue again. Keisha followed his instructions and went home. She took two days off and went in to see if they could reach a resolution. When she arrived, she was greeted with a completely different scenario...none of the managers wanted to discuss anything with Keisha. Every attempt she made to speak with someone resulted in waiting for a manager to be available while she sat off to the side, as if she didn't know what kind of games they were playing...they were all avoiding her.

Finally, one of Keisha's coworkers who she was close with, called her into the back office and told her they were stalling to talk to her because they were preparing her separation notice. Keisha was floored! She could not believe that they were giving her the runaround just so they could lie and say that she 'abandoned her job'. She couldn't believe that she was being forced into this position, but she was not going to back down and go along with whatever they said just to keep a job. At this point, she did what she had to do and filed unemployment. Although her claim was initially denied, Keisha was awarded unemployment after she appealed the denial. One of the main reasons she won her appeal was due to a lack of evidence to back their claim of 'job abandonment'. She was happy she stood up for herself and won the case, but she was pissed that her plans were interrupted. She still had 11 months to reach her savings and business goals.

This drastic adjustment made it difficult for Keisha to stay focused on her plan for her entrepreneurial journey She was jolted back into being unemployed and struggling to make her dreams come true. Although she was going to receive unemployment, she knew she wouldn't make the type of money she needed to make. She was going to have to rob Peter to pay Paul and still barely make ends meet. A part of her felt like if Tyler would just help her financially, she wouldn't have such a hard time. She felt like it would have been a bit more manageable if he would help consistently or if she didn't have to always make these types of adjustments. She just wanted Tyler to help her care for and raise the same children he had a hand in making.

Every time she went to back to these thoughts, she felt like a failure. She felt like she was always making the right decision at the wrong time. A fragment of her felt like she would be able to cry about it, get it out, and move on. Keisha gathered all the parts of herself and attempted to piece the woman she currently was with the woman she wanted to be.

Losing this job was a catalyst for her. As the part of her that wanted to cry and move on continued to grow and flourish, the more she fought through the struggle. She felt like she was getting stronger and stronger after every obstacle, but she did not like the feeling of this growth process. Regardless of how strong she felt, she still was not where she wanted to be financially. Keisha was having trouble sustaining herself and the kids on the money she was receiving. Although she was looking for other work, her options were very limited. She was hoping that filing bankruptcy would be a helpful step as she continued to move forward.

After she filed, she had a sense of relief. She felt like it was something she probably should have done sooner. Nevertheless, it was a smart move for her based on her current status. Since most of her money was freed up through the bankruptcy, she started paying on the bills she had left. She drafted a new plan so she could get closer to living her dreams. In Keisha's mind, because of the bankruptcy, she was able to take this opportunity to reset. Her landlord had other plans in mind. He started giving her a hard time about the rent, the lawn, and the repairs she requested to have done. He even started to pop up at Keisha's house unannounced at random times of day. It was safe to assume that Keisha was being watched based on the actions of her landlord.

A few days later, there was an influx of media coverage about police brutality against black people. Keisha knew this type of stuff was going on because it happened to someone in her family years ago. Now, due to the popularity of social media, it was being thrown in the face of society and it seemed as if all anyone could do was stand by and watch. It shook Keisha up and she felt like she had to do something. As a mother with black children, living in a subpar neighborhood, she was naturally concerned about the safety of her own children. She made two small signs that read 'BLACK LIVES MATTER' and placed them in her interior window. A few hours after she put the signs up, the landlord called and told her to remove them.

Keisha was so confused. She had no clue who saw the signs and reported them to the landlord. It wasn't like she was spewing hate speech or something. It didn't make sense. Why was having these signs such a big deal? How could someone see these and be offended? Why was somebody looking so hard at what Keisha was doing? None of it made sense. The signs were in the front window, but the window was primary blocked by a large bush. So, someone would have had to be fairly close to her front door to see the signs.

Keisha checked her lease and read a clause that vaguely mentioned 'only approved signs' can be erected by residents. Keisha felt like she was being targeted at this point. Instead of taking the signs completely down, she moved them to another area in her house. She also put up some holiday signs to see if she would be directed to take those down as well. Nothing was ever said about the holiday signs, but the landlord threatened to evict Keisha if she put up any other signs like 'BLACK LIVES MATTER' again. She was furious! She could not believe that he was able to get away with this. Keisha was being treated like a criminal for putting these signs up, meanwhile, the repairs in the unit were still incomplete.

Keisha started to put in more and more requests for repairs. Every time she did, she was met with a reason why her request could not be fulfilled quickly. The landlord was evidently treating Keisha differently. As contractors came in to finally complete the repairs, they gave Keisha an ear full of information every single visit. They told her how shady the landlords were, how many properties they owned and how they did just enough to patch the problem. They told Keisha they were not supposed to actually fix something unless it couldn't be patched up well enough to operate. It was torture to hear this. Keisha thought she was moving to a place to help save money and improve her situation, but it was turning out to be one of the worst moves ever.

The following week, Keisha received three envelopes from Social Security. Two envelopes held checks that totaled just over $6,000 and a letter explaining why she was receiving the checks. According to the letter, Tyler was awarded Social Security disability benefits and these checks were for the back pay that each child was entitled to as a result. The other envelope had a letter explaining why there was no back payment check for Heaven. Her letter stated that they would review her case to see if she was entitled to anything since she was receiving SSI due to her own disability.

Keisha couldn't explain how grateful she was to have this blessing. The timing of receiving this money was perfect because she would now be able to provide for herself and her children a hell of a lot better than before. Although the major bills were gone with the bankruptcy, Keisha needed a new vehicle and had some bills that she still had to catch up on. Had she known this lump sum of money would trigger the next wave of events, she would have used it differently. A week after the checks cleared, Keisha received a call from Judy telling her to report what she received to child support enforcement. As a result of this massive payment, Tyler and Keisha would have to undergo a child support review to assess where they stood.

Keisha thought this review would work in her favor, especially since Tyler was still so deep in arrears inconsistent with payments. The judge was the one with the most control in this situation. He was the deciding factor on how this credit would be applied to the account. There were three options on how to apply the credit. The first option is to apply the credit when the youngest child is about to age out of receiving payments. This option was the most common option. The second option was to apply the credit to the account immediately which would mean no child support payments from Tyler. The third option was to do what the court calls 'split the baby'. This option was a mix of the first two. If the third option was selected, Tyler would be responsible for paying half of the child support amount each month and the credit would be applied to the other half of the payment.

Option three seemed like the only logical option for Keisha and that's what she opted for. When the review was done, Keisha learned that Tyler would receive a full credit on his child support account effective immediately. This meant that he would have the amount of the disability back pay checks deducted from what he was required to pay each month. In short, Tyler wouldn't have to pay child support until this 'credit' was depleted which equated to about 4 years. Keisha was devastated! She felt like the judge ignored the needs of the kids and the struggle Keisha was experiencing to give Tyler yet another break.

Something just did not sit right with her. Why would the

judge give him the credit now? Tyler was remarried and was evidently more stable and secure than Keisha. In her mind, it didn't make sense! This was the final straw for Keisha! After the hearing was done, Judy told Keisha she could no longer help her unless she rehired her as her attorney. On one hand, it seemed like Murphy's Law was laying the smack down on Keisha, but on the other hand, she felt like this was her time to stop being a victim and start being a survivor. Keisha went home and closed the doors, got in the shower, and screamed. She cried and screamed for about 5 minutes. She was full of so many emotions and she didn't know how else to release them in that moment. When she got out of the shower, she felt refreshed and refocused.

She returned to promoting her business and working towards her goals. She invested in a few business ventures that seemed to be lucrative options at the time. She didn't completely know how she was going to manage her life, but she knew she was going to make something happen. She took this hit on the chin and used it as motivation. She started spending more money on things for the kids and let them get involved in whatever activities they wanted to participate in. When her lease was up, she took the opportunity to relocate. She believed that the more she could expose her children to, the more opportunities they would have. One of her goals was to make sure that she nor her children would end up as statistics. Keisha wanted them to have more than what she had and more than they would ever need.

When they moved this time, it was a much better situation. It was the start of the new life they deserved. Keisha and her friend, Tammie, decided to go into business together.

They created a branding and marketing company that would produce continual clients, countless income, and franchise opportunities. They started by servicing the needs of the sports team their children were on and it the business took off! Keisha and Tammie were both single mothers who wanted to change the lives of their children. They worked hard and rarely took breaks. They were always looking for ways to improve branding and marketing for their business.

Within the first 6 months, they had to rent office space to handle all the business they had! For Keisha and Tammie, this was a major accomplishment! A year before, they were both struggling and had no idea how they were going to get ahead...but now, they were both working diligently to create new lives and were focused on changing the narrative they were initially given. To see harvest of their hard work in real life was a beautiful sight. They were proud of what they had achieved, and they looked forward to continuing to grow. The kids were even getting involved in the business. While these were the moments that Keisha longed for, they were actually more than she had ever imagined. Before they knew it, their business was booming! Local and distant business owners were contacting them for their services. Their name was making its way around the city and surrounding areas, and it was amazing! Keisha was extremely proud. She was happy to say that she and Tammie were successful businesswomen. When Keisha felt some of the pressure ease up, she started to give more attention to her mental health as their rising success continued.

CHAPTER TWELVE

The Hunt Continues

Mental health was important to Keisha. She knew how it felt to drown in her thoughts instead of swim through them. She never wanted to get to a place like that again. The fact that things were going so well for Keisha and Tammie made it easier to properly care for her mental well-being. Aside from that, the most peaceful feeling in the world was that Keisha no longer needed Tyler. At this point in her life, she was operating a successful business with Tammie and working on publishing more books. She was no longer controlled by Tyler's decisions. Keisha and Tammie were able to be the type of mothers they longed to be for their children. They did not have to struggle to 'figure it out' or 'barely get by' anymore.

Keisha was proud of what she and Tammie built. Keisha desired this moment for so long and she was determined not to allow Tyler to dictate her life. In the midst of Keisha celebrating her accomplishments, she received a letter from child support enforcement. The letter stated it was time for a case review. It went on to say that neither party needed to be present for the review and if they chose not to attend, they would receive the results of the review in the mail. Keisha didn't sweat it. A few weeks went by, and the child support enforcement office notified both Keisha and Tyler that the amount of support would increase due to the amount of money Tyler was bringing in monthly. This didn't sit well with Tyler so he requested an appeal hearing.

The hearing was scheduled six weeks after they were notified. When the time came to go to the hearing, Keisha prepared herself for the worst. She didn't know what would happen, but she expected Tyler to have some sort of trick up his sleeve. Nevertheless, Keisha went to the hearing alone. She paced the courtroom lobby for roughly 30 minutes waiting for Tyler to show up. When the case was called, she was confused because Tyler was not there. Before she could formulate too many questions, she heard a voice speak.

"I'm here for Tyler as his representative Your Honor." Tyler's lawyer said. "I'll have my client on the phone during the proceedings if you need to speak with him directly Your Honor." His lawyer continued.

A weight was lifted off Keisha's shoulders, but she couldn't understand why Tyler needed his lawyer to be there for him. The hearing started and the judge asked Tyler why he felt the new amount was unfair.

"Well, me and my wife have 5 kids so we can't afford to pay what the court suggests and still maintain our home." Tyler said from his lawyer's phone.

The judge asked for proof that Tyler was on the birth certificates of all 5 children. His lawyer requested a quick recess to get the documents. Tyler sent over birth certificates and his lawyer gave them to the judge.

"Well Tyler, there are only four birth certificates in here. Is there a reason why all five were not sent?" The judge asked.

"Your honor, initially, I was not listed on my first son's birth certificate Your Honor. That is why we did not include it. A DNA test was done to confirm that he is my son, but we didn't put my name on the birth certificate cause we weren't married yet." Tyler explained.

Tyler seemed to have muted the phone because he was deathly silent all of a sudden. The judge asked if them having 5 kids is why he wasn't in attendance. Tyler told the judge that they relocated to Texas, and it was too difficult to get there. The judge asked Tyler about his disability payments and the amount of each one. Tyler gave him the total and it was more than what Keisha made in a month just in disability payments. At this point, Tyler still wasn't paying child support due to his previous credit, but the increased amount would reduce the credit quickly and the child support payments would have to start back soon.

This is not what Tyler wanted at all. Although Keisha did not have a lawyer, the child support enforcement agency had a legal representative to assist her. He advised her to request to 'split the baby'. Keisha took the advice and told the judge when he asked her. She was a little concerned about how this would turn out since it didn't go so well the last time. The judge considered the amount of children Tyler and Maria had when he raised the new amount Tyler would have to pay. Keisha still felt like Tyler was getting leniency but this time it was different.

After the hearing, Keisha was understandably annoyed. However, she felt like Tyler was running out of tricks and he couldn't hurt her or the kids anymore. The only thing he could do was pay what he was told to pay. One thing

Keisha learned during the hearing was that Tyler was receiving 100% disability from Veteran Affairs and was not allowed to control his finances without the assistance and guidance of a lawyer. Once he received the 100% disabled veteran status from the VA, Social Security awarded him disability automatically. Since the judge agreed to the 'split the baby' option, he ordered Tyler to start making payments of $400 per month starting the following month.

After a few months of regular support payments, Keisha received a letter in the mail from the Social Security office. The letter stated that Heaven's supplemental security income would be reduced because she receives money from VA. Immediately Keisha called the social security office to find out what they were referring to. When she spoke to the agent, they told her that the Veteran benefits the children received would impact any additional income, including SSI. Keisha was confused. She had no idea what this agent was talking about. This wasn't making any sense. Keisha was told that VA and Social Security have connected systems and they report to each other about benefits. Based on what the information the VA gave, Heaven's SSI payments would be reduced by nearly $100 per month.

Granted, Keisha was not struggling the way she was in the past, she still did not like the idea of money being taken from Heaven for benefits that she was not receiving. Keisha told the Social Security agent that Heaven does not receive VA benefits. The agent told Keisha to contact VA and get proof because someone was receiving benefits for her. Keisha could not bring herself to stress over more of Tyler's shenanigans. She just did what she needed to do to prove that Heaven wasn't receiving the benefits. Keisha called VA and informed the representative of the issue. The representative informed Keisha that Tyler was receiving benefits on behalf of the children and that is why it was reported to Social Security.

Keisha explained that they are not together, and he is not in the home with his oldest three children that he was receiving benefits for. Since the benefits were not coming directly to Heaven, the representative was able to give Keisha a letter stating that their children do not receive VA benefits. Keisha asked if the benefits could go directly to the children instead of Tyler and she learned that they could, but it would take a lot of work. She was told to file an apportionment request. Keisha submitted the request and received a letter stating that she filled out the wrong form for the request and gave her the correct form number to use. Without hesitation, Keisha completed the correct form and resubmitted.

Keisha received a response stating that the apportionment was denied, and she could file an appeal...so she did. During the appeal process, Tyler would have an opportunity to explain why the apportionment should be denied just as she had to explain why it should be granted. A few weeks went by, and Keisha received a letter stating the denial is final as Tyler would not be able to sustain if he gives the money to their children. The letter went on to say that if Keisha was still dissatisfied with the decision, she could write to her congressman to get him involved.

Keisha wrote 3 separate letters to her congressman and only received blanket responses and generic letters in return. The more of a fuss she caused, the more it seemed like she was ignored. At one point, she was told that since Tyler 'takes care of his children', he is not required to give them the benefits he receives for them, even the ones that he had no contact with. Every step of the process was so disheartening. It was like she was always three steps behind whatever Tyler was doing. She felt like he had help...like someone knew what to say and what to do all the time. It was one of the hardest things for Keisha to do but she decided to give up in that moment.

She wanted this to be over so long ago, and it was still dragging on years later. In her mind, no matter what she did, Tyler would always get his way. So, she quit fighting. She gave up and stopped giving energy to Tyler and his wife. She knew that she needed to stay focused on her new life and new goals. Keisha fought so long and so hard to create a better life for her and her children despite what Tyler and Maria had going on. She gave up on understanding how Maria could walk in her home and shake her hand knowing that she's in a secret love affair with Tyler. Keisha knew that Maria and Tyler's oldest son was conceived when Tyler was still married to Keisha. This was the final straw for Keisha. After so many years of dealing with his mess, she finally started living as if Tyler did not exist.

It was the best decision she made since all of this began. She finally started to live the life she wanted...completely unrestricted and unbothered! She stopped thinking that Tyler could control what she was doing. She saw how important it was to be present with her children. She realized just how much she had survived through. For years Keisha attempted to figure out why...Why did this have to happen to her? Why did she allow this to be her life? Why did it end the way it did? Why did Tyler's family walk away from the kids?...and so on and so on. She had so many questions with few to no answers. Nevertheless, she made it! She did not succumb to the negative thoughts that seeped into her mind. She did not give up! Most of this journey, Keisha had gone through alone but she vowed that from now on, she would not only speak up but speak out about what she felt and knew to be right.

Keisha kept writing through all her trials and challenges and started a blog to share her thoughts about random life situations. She wrote about things she experienced and lessons she learned along the way. Her goal was to help others to tell their story and obtain whatever they needed from the process, whether it be healing, resources, or just strength. At that point, Keisha wanted to make a difference. She wanted to stand up for those suffering in silence. She knew what it was like to be alone and did not want that to be that case for others if she could help it. As a result, Keisha decided to start a non-profit organization to help others who may be experiencing the same things she survived.

She had an idea to create a community to assist domestic violence survivors, recently divorced, former military, and poverty-stricken families. She wanted to give them the tools they needed to adjust to the new world around them with little to no stress about finances, housing, food, education, counseling, or other major necessities. She wanted to be able to provide everything someone would need to transition from one shift in their life to another. She wanted to give the steppingstones to turn survivors into thrivers. She created an acronym for the organization but could not think of what she wanted it to stand for. She called her sister to tell her about the idea. While they were talking, it came to her. It was the perfect name for her non-profit. It represented everything that Keisha wanted to do to help others.

When she announced what she was doing to the rest of her family and friends, they were immediately on board. It felt so good to speak out about what she'd gone through. Keisha was so grateful for her survival and her sanity. She was amazed at how easy it was to get others involved with her vision. Before she knew it, Keisha was more than she ever dreamed of being. Her success was measured in moments of happiness. Being an author, mom, businesswoman, and non-profit founder made Keisha very happy and thus very successful. During one of her community events, Keisha was introduced to Edmond Jones. He was a well-known figure in the community and he had heard a lot about what Keisha was doing and decided to get involved.

This was a major game changer for Keisha. She was suddenly at events with people she only imagined being around. Edmond was able to open doors for Keisha that she didn't even know she wanted to walk through. It was so refreshing to meet someone with a similar passion and drive for helping others. They developed an amazing friendship while working with one another. Soon, it became the norm to see them together. Neither of them expected it but it was the beautiful surprise that they both needed. Edmond was very supportive of Keisha's writing and always encouraged her to write more. He was fascinated by her skills and wanted to be involved in her future projects. He saw something special in Keisha and wanted to do whatever he could to ensure her continued success.

Over the course of the next year, Keisha wrote another

book and started another business. Everything was falling into place. Keisha watched her children grow from small little babies into wonderfully awesome teenagers. They were so inspired by everything their mom accomplished that they decided to take more active roles in her non-profit. It was wonderful to see them as strong, young adults despite all that they went through. Keisha knew she deserved more and as a result, so did her children. When she decided to step out and live life against the grain, it was a major challenge. She made it to the other side with style and poise. She was twisted, bent, and pulled in all directions and forced to overcome some crazy obstacles, but she made it! Keisha did not stay down, and she didn't give up. She kept going and created the life she always knew she deserved. For Keisha this wasn't a happy ending, but it was one dope ass new beginning!

www.ingramcontent.com/pod-product-compliance
Lightning Source LLC
Chambersburg PA
CBHW040933030426
42336CB00006B/64